if it falls on the floor, it's mine

a cookbook recommended by three 100-pound lap dogs, sampled by a wonderful husband and fed to some great neighbors and friends!

Megan E. McFarlane

with a lot of tasting from Malcolm
and a lot of floor licking & chomping at the
crumbs from the girls

Happy tail wags!

i

ISBN-13: 978-0615869827 (If It Falls on the Floor It's Mine LLC)
ISBN-10: 0615869823

Photography: Megan and Malcolm McFarlane

Publisher
IF IT FALLS ON THE FLOOR, IT'S MINE LLC

www.ifitfallsonthefloor.com

Edits and formatting by Ruth Andrews. Cover by Cristina Arnal.

Dedicated to the memory of Sam

who adored Tiamo and would eat anything I
cooked for him, along with the stray dog hair

miss you kiddo!

Counter-surfing the contents

i melt butter and hearts!

PREFACE

In my past life, I owned a catering business where people often asked me how I learned to cook.

My father, a cattle rancher from the central coast of California, was one of the originators of the "Santa Maria-style BBQ" back in the 1950s. He was fortunate to be able to combine his love of food with his gift for gab; weekends often included invitations to dinner for friends and neighbors. Dad would barbeque his famous beef tri-tips and mother would put us kids to work in the kitchen, making salads, beans and casseroles. It was the start of my cooking lessons.

Years later, I started catering on my own and opened my business, Divine Bovine. I custom-catered small cocktail parties, fancy galas, annual dinners, intimate dinners for two and fundraising events for 750 attendees. I catered lunch for Al Gore, then Vice President of the United States; other congressmen and political hopefuls; Steve Young, quarterback for the San Francisco 49ers; Dave Dravecky, who played for the San Francisco Giants, and a very close friend of Julia Child. I gave cooking lessons to children and taught classes for adults, all with standing room only. Rarely did I serve the same entrée twice.

Three file cabinets crammed with recipes and 237 cookbooks later, I closed my catering business, married the love of my life and moved to New Mexico. I swore I would never work nights, weekends or holidays again.

Little did I know how that would change the minute I gave my husband a Bernese Mountain Dog puppy for his 50th birthday. Named Tiamo, the newest member of our family had us wrapped around every one of her paws within five minutes of bringing her home. Every day was an adventure for Tiamo: there were books to chew, magazines to rip up and wooden spoons to carry from room to room. Friends would fight over who held Tiamo's leash on walks. Neighborhood kids would randomly drop by to pet her. She was the darling of the community and our hearts.

Tiamo knew not to beg for table scraps, but she was quick to lick up any tasty tidbit that fell to the floor. We learned Tiamo had a keen ability to counter-surf, quickly and quietly. Cartons of cream would go missing, only to be found empty in another room. Cookies cooling on racks would be one fewer of a dozen. Licked-clean butter plates would be discovered under couch pillows. Then she was busted — caught in the act with one paw reaching for the goods! At two in the morning, we were awakened by a big crash; Tiamo had crawled up on the kitchen table to lick up crumbs. Anyone who has ever owned a dog has had a similar experience: turning your back for just a few minutes while cooking, resulting in missing ingredients and a look from your pooch that says, "Who, me?"

My love of cooking for family, friends, and my enjoyment of Tiamo's humorous antics while sniffing for a fallen crumb has produced a cookbook designed to bring compliments to the chef and smiles from the cook, along with a tasty morsel for your dog.

Yes, cooking and dogs do go together - they are both joyous! And a stray dog hair is a reminder of their unconditional love.

the McFarlane pack...

People often ask us how we tell the "girls" apart. Sometimes even we get confused.

Of course, this usually resulted in Dolce being accused of something Amore did or Tiamo getting away with a no-no. When they were puppies, we never knew which one had committed the crime. Today we know they are all in cahoots together.

Tiamo, the mother, had a deep-barreled chest and a more queenly stature. She had a prance in her walk, like a model walking down the catwalk. She will always be our "girl."

Amore has a bit more spice in her personality. Always on the go, always has to run. She is the one who gulps her food down the fastest and the one who has seen the vet's office the most.

Dolce is our sweetheart. With a thin white stripe on her forehead and almost no white on her tail, Dolce likes to hang with the old folks but is always first out the door and in the car.

... So, if you don't know which dog is with you, just love the one you're with.

a calm moment before chaos erupts!

Never feed or let your pet eat avocados, baby food, mushrooms, chocolate, grapes, raisins, garlic, onions, chives, leeks, chile, walnuts, macadamia nuts, alcohol, caffeinated beverages, bread dough, mints, sugar-free gum, gum with artificial sweetener Xylitol, rock salt, lilies, poinsettias, hyacinth, chamomile, carnations, baby's breath, bulbs (such as tulips, daffodils, hyacinth), aloe and/or anything that could be potentially harmful to your pet.

"it tastes better straight from the can" – amore

"i wanted more!" – amore

always start with a drink in hand

Most times, dinner parties start with cocktails and appetizers. Upon arrival, guests are asked, "what can I get you to drink?" Glasses are filled with ice and beverages are poured. Inevitably, some ice will fall to the floor – not to worry, the dogs will munch on the cubes. These hot and cold drink recipes are perfect any time of the year!

it started with tiamo...

SANTA FE SANGRIA
guaranteed to make your spouse agreeable

1 bottle of dry red wine (3 c)
1½ c 7UP soda
1½ c orange juice
16 lemon slices & 16 lime slices (save 8 of each for the glass garnish)
8 orange slices
½ c brandy
¼ c sugar
2 tbsp. Cointreau or orange liqueur
2 tbsp. grenadine
2 tbsp. lemon juice & 2 tbsp. lime juice
ice

Mix all together. Fill 8 large wineglasses with ice. Divide sangria among the glasses. Garnish with remaining lemon and lime slices.

"its good, but not as good as cold toilet water" - tiamo

SLUGGIN' IT DOWN SLUGGERS

1 c freshly brewed strong coffee
¼ c bourbon
1-2 tbsp. Kahlua
2 oz. finely chopped bittersweet chocolate (not unsweetened)
6 tbsp. heavy cream
1 tsp. sugar

Heat coffee, bourbon, Kahlua, chocolate and 2 tbsp. of cream in a 2-quart heavy saucepan over low heat, whisking constantly, until chocolate is melted (about 2-4 minutes). Do not let it boil. Beat remaining ¼ cup cream with sugar until it holds soft peaks. Divide mixture into coffee mugs and top with whipped cream. Serve on a snowy, lazy day with a roaring fire.

"i like licking the coffee rings left on the end table, even though I'm not supposed to!" – amore

CAIPIRINHAS

Peel the green rind from 4 large limes into 2-inch-long strips
1 c fresh lime juice
8 (¼-inch-thick) slices of peeled fresh ginger
¼ c sugar
30 large fresh mint leaves + 10 mint sprigs for garnish

1 c rum
3 c ice cubes
5 c ginger beer or ginger ale

Combine the lime peel, ginger, sugar and 30 mint leaves in medium bowl. Using the handle of a wooden spoon, crush lime peel, ginger and mint leaves together. Add lime juice and mix well. Transfer mixture to large pitcher. Add the rum. Cover and refrigerate. To serve, stir in ginger beer or ginger ale. Fill cocktail glasses with ice cubes and pour. Garnish with mint sprig.

"ginger... ick!" – the girls

MALCOLM'S SOUTHERN SWEET TEA
who needs a recipe for tea? In my husband's opinion, damn near everyone!

My poor aggrieved husband has suffered many a terrible glass of ice tea. In view of his long suffering, he has provided the ultimate answer....

1 qt. cold water (vital in his opinion)
2 qts. cold water, filtered (set aside)
2 c brown sugar
5 tea bags
lemon wedges
mint leaves (optional)

Bring 1 quart cold water to boil. As you wait, take your finest pitcher of 3-quart capacity and add the brown sugar. In a separate glass container, pour the boiling water over tea bags. Let steep for 4 minutes - time it! Immediately pour brewed tea into pitcher with brown sugar and stir to dissolve sugar. Add the cold filtered water. The golden ratio is 2:1, water to steeped tea.

Fill glass to brim with shaved ice (Malcolm's preferred style of ice) and squeeze lemon wedges over ice. Pour in tea.

If desired, run the rim of the glass with crushed mint leaves. Enjoy with the dogs!

"we get lots of love, once malcolm has had his iced tea!" – the girls

dolce after a fun day playing in the paw pool

COFFEE EGGNOG
perfect for the holidays

2 c freshly brewed dark coffee, cooled
2 c prepared eggnog
1 – 8-oz. tub of whipped topping, thawed
½ tsp. ground cinnamon
½ c rum or brandy
ground nutmeg

Mix coffee, eggnog, half the whipped topping and cinnamon in a large pitcher. Add rum and stir. Keep in the refrigerator until ready to serve.

Pour into glasses, top each glass with a dollop of whipped topping and sprinkle with nutmeg. Lick whipped topping off spoon before placing in dishwasher.

WARNING: easy to drink too many of these!

SANTA FE CAPPUCCINO

hot coffee
steamed milk
Kahlua

cinnamon stick for garnish

Pour hot coffee into a mug and add Kahlua and steamed milk. Add the cinnamon stick and serve.

"rats! all the things we can't have" – the girls

Working up an appetite! Malcolm and dolce breaking trail

Tiamo...

Born on Thanksgiving, Tiamo was a birthday gift to my husband when he turned 50. Within minutes, she had Malcolm and I wrapped around every one of her paws. Life as we knew it just changed ... and Malcolm's hair just turned gray!

Tiamo was our everywhere dog. Wherever we went, she went. People adored her, we just plain loved her.

When we bred her, the whole neighborhood was part of the pregnancy. At four weeks, she had a sonogram, which revealed four puppies – she had eight! Every night during her pregnancy, I gave Tiamo belly rubs, a ritual that continued on a daily basis ever since. Tiamo was a great mom!

Tiamo was our "dog" clock. She let us know when it was time to walk, to eat and to go to sleep. At 5:10 p.m. on the dot, she wanted to be let out in the front portal to wait for me to arrive home from work. At 8:30 p.m., she came down to the den and barked, telling me it was time for me to come to bed. She knew when the mailman arrived and she always knew when something "good" might be cooking!

Somehow we ended up with two of her puppies, Amore and Dolce, enriching our lives even more. Although raising two puppies and mom was quite an adventure, we wouldn't trade it for a single minute!

"woof, woof, time for our walk! woof, come on! woof, NOW!" - tiamo

megs and tiamo

peanut butter kongs
otherwise known as appetizers!

"WOW!" "These are fantastic!" "How did you make them?" These comments I guarantee the cook will hear when serving these tasty nibbles. Tried and true appetizers from my catering days, these appetizers may be served as hearty tidbits or as a first course. As the girls will testify, anything with peanut butter is great.

dolce, not caring that dinner is in 5 minutes

JOSEPHINA'S

1 sourdough baguette loaf
1 – 4-oz. can Hatch chopped green chile, or more for a spicier taste
¼ lb. butter, softened (1 stick)
1 c mayonnaise
2 minced garlic cloves
½ lb. Monterey Jack or Cheddar cheese, grated
1/8 c minced parsley

Slice the bread and set aside and out of reach from any paw. Mix the rest of the ingredients until thoroughly blended. Spread mixture on the sliced bread and place on a baking sheet.

May be frozen at this point. You may substitute green onions for the green chile.

Preheat oven to broil. Broil until bubbly and just starting to brown. Serve immediately.

TEXAS TACO TARTS

1 1/3 lb. lean ground beef
2 tbsp. taco seasoning mix
2 tbsp. ice-cold water
1 pint sour cream
2 tbsp. taco sauce or green salsa
2 oz. chopped ripe black olives
1 c crushed tortilla chips
8 oz. grated Cheddar cheese

Preheat oven to 425°F. Using hands to mix, combine ground beef, taco seasoning and water. Press beef mixture into the bottom and sides of a greased mini muffin pan.

Mix sour cream, salsa, olives and chips together. Place a spoonful of filling mixture into each beef shell. Sprinkle Cheddar cheese over top and bake for 8-10 minutes. With the tip of a knife, remove tart and place on paper towel to drain off extra grease. Serve warm. Count the number of tarts on the platter – you might be short one.

"dear God, please let some hamburger drop to the floor, AMEN!" – the dog congregation

PESTO PINWHEELS

1 package puff pastry
1 – 8-oz. jar pesto or use recipe below
1 c Parmesan cheese, divided in half
1 egg, beaten

Thaw pastry sheets (approx. 20 minutes). Roll out the puff pastry sheets to a rectangle about 11 inches x 14 inches in size.

Spread half the pesto on the pastry sheet, leaving a ½-inch margin on the edges. Sprinkle ½ cup of Parmesan cheese on the pesto.

Starting with the long edge, carefully roll the pesto/cheese-stuffed puff pastry sheet, keeping the roll tight. Brush the beaten egg on the seam of the pastry sheet to seal. Repeat the process with the other puff pastry sheet. Wrap tight with plastic wrap and freeze.

When ready to use, remove from freezer and slice the pastry roll into ¼-inch rounds. Place on an ungreased baking sheet and bake at 400°F for 10-15 minutes or until puffy and golden brown. Serve warm.

HOMEMADE PESTO

2 c fresh basil leaves
2 cloves garlic
¾ c Parmesan cheese, grated
½ c pine nuts
2/3 c olive oil

Place basil leaves and garlic in food processor or blender. Process until mixture is pureed. Add Parmesan cheese and pine nuts. Continue blending until smooth. While processor is running, slowly add olive oil and continue running until combined. Freeze extra pesto sauce in ice-cube trays.
12 pesto cubes = 1 cup approximately.

"mmm, basil - i'll pass" - tiamo

PESTO STUFFED MUSHROOMS

2 cartons mushrooms (medium sized)
8 oz. cream cheese, softened
3 oz. pesto sauce (recipe on page 13)
1¼ c mozzarella cheese, grated

Preheat oven to 350°F. Wash mushrooms and carefully remove stems. Flip upside down to dry. Fill mushroom cavity with cream cheese and top with pesto sauce. Sprinkle with mozzarella cheese. Bake for 10-12 minutes or until the cheese starts to melt. Serve hot.

"mushrooms are ok, but we'd rather have the cheese" – the girls

TEX-MEX CAVIAR
Perfect for a large crowd or BBQ

½ c yellow onion, chopped
2 medium tomatoes, diced
4 green onions, diced
2 garlic cloves, minced
1 green pepper, chopped
2 jalapenos, minced
½ c cilantro, minced

Mix all ingredients together in a large glass bowl. Add the following:

2 – 14-oz. cans black-eyed peas, drained
1 – 30-oz. can white hominy (washed and drained)
1 – 8-oz. bottle low-fat Italian dressing

Mix until blended. Chill. Best if made a day ahead of time. Serve with corn chips.

pleeease, I want some!

ARTICHOKE CROWNS

16 oz. cream cheese, softened
1 small package of ranch-style dressing seasoning
8 oz. Parmesan cheese, grated
water-packed artichoke crowns (otherwise known as Artichoke Bottoms)

Mix together the cream cheese and ranch dressing dip mix until thoroughly blended, making sure mixture is smooth. Set aside in the refrigerator.

Rinse artichoke crowns and pat dry. Arrange crowns on a baking sheet. Pipe a rosette of the cream cheese mixture onto the crowns. Sprinkle with Parmesan cheese. Bake at 375°F for 5–10 minutes or until Parmesan begins to brown.

BLTs
Pop-in-your-mouth delicious

1 carton cherry tomatoes
1 lb. bacon, cut into 1-inch pieces
¼ c sour cream
¼ c mayonnaise (may substitute plain yogurt)
4 green onions, minced

Cut a thin slice off the bottoms of the tomatoes. With a small scoop, remove the centers of the tomatoes and place upside down on paper towels to drain and dry.

Fry the bacon pieces until crispy. Place on a paper towel to absorb the grease. Pat dry. Chop bacon into small bits. Hide until ready to use.

Mix the bacon, sour cream, mayonnaise and green onions together. Stuff the cherry tomatoes with the bacon mixture. Place on a serving tray and refrigerate until ready to serve.

WARNING: hide the bacon!

bummmer man, there's never enough leftovers

SHRIMP AND BLEU CHEESE

this is a showstopper of a dish, and it's delicious too!

24 large shrimp (cooked, shelled & deveined)
3 oz. cream cheese, softened
1 oz. bleu cheese crumbles
1 tsp. prepared mustard
1 tsp. finely chopped green onions
1 c finely chopped fresh parsley

Butterfly the shrimp down the spine of its back about halfway through. Set aside in the refrigerator.

Mix cream cheese, bleu cheese, mustard and onions until well blended. Using a piping bag or small spatula, carefully fill the butterflied split of the shrimp with the cream cheese mixture. Roll the cream cheese side of the shrimp in the chopped parsley. Chill until ready to serve.

CRAB TRIANGLES

8 oz. crabmeat
8 oz. cream cheese, softened
1 tsp. steak sauce
1/2 tsp. garlic powder
1 package wonton skins
water to moisten edges
peanut oil for frying

Mix together crabmeat, cream cheese, and steak sauce and garlic powder. Place one teaspoon of mixture onto each wonton skin.

Moisten two adjacent edges with water and fold opposite corners together, making a triangle. Seal edges. Place in a single layer in frying pan coated with 1/2 inch of hot peanut oil. Fry until golden brown on one side and turn over on other side. Place on a paper towel to absorb extra oil. Serve warm.

"Crab scraps! YIPPEE!" - amore

amore running in for dinner
100 pounds of dog stopping 1/16 of an inch from your knees

MARINATED GARLIC OLIVES

¼ c olive oil
¼ c red wine vinegar
2 tbsp. fresh chives, chopped

1 tsp. paprika
3 garlic cloves, minced
2 – 16-oz. cans pitted black olives, drained

In a large glass bowl, mix together the first five ingredients. Place olives in mixture, cover and marinate in refrigerator for 2 to 3 days, stirring occasionally.

"nothing here worth investigating" - tiamo

MARINATED GARLIC AND GOAT CHEESE

2 large garlic heads
16 oz. olive oil
11 oz. log of Montrachet goat cheese

1½ tbsp.-dried rosemary
2 bay leaves
1 tbsp. black peppercorns

Carefully separate garlic head into cloves. Peel and place garlic cloves in a small saucepan, adding just enough olive oil to cover the bottom of the pan. Cook very slowly over low heat until garlic cloves soften. If garlic cooks too quickly or browns, the garlic will be bitter. Remove from heat and cool in pan.

Slice goat cheese in 1-inch rounds. Place in a crock or jar with a tight-fitting lid. Add remaining olive oil, herbs, pepper and cooled garlic with the oil.

Cover and leave at room temperature for 24 hours. Store in refrigerator for up to 2 weeks. Serve at room temperature with toasted French bread crisps.

"can't have garlic!" - the girls

all is well – a rare quiet moment with amore

FRESH ASPARAGUS

2 lbs. fresh asparagus, trimmed

Bring a big pot of salted water to boil. Place asparagus in boiling water for 2-3 minutes. Remove from water immediately and place in ice-cold water to stop the cooking process.

Serve chilled with a dipping sauce from below.

WARM GORGONZOLA DIP

7 slices bacon, diced
2 garlic cloves, minced
8 oz. cream cheese, softened
¼ c half and half cream

4 oz. Gorgonzola cheese crumbles
2 tbsp. fresh parsley, chopped
3 tbsp. almonds (smoked ok), chopped

Cook bacon in a heavy skillet until almost crisp; drain off excess grease. Add garlic and cook until bacon is crispy. Using a food processor, beat cream cheese until smooth. Add half and half and continue to beat until blended. Stir in bacon and garlic, Gorgonzola and parsley.

Transfer to an ovenproof dish and bake at 350°F until heated through, about 30 minutes. Sprinkle with the chopped almonds.

HERBED CAPER DIPPING SAUCE

8 oz. cream cheese
½ c sour cream
3 scallions, minced
2 tbsp. capers

2 tbsp. Dijon mustard
2 tbsp. parsley, minced
1 tsp. herbes de Provence
salt and pepper to taste

Beat cream cheese and sour cream until light and fluffy. Stir in remaining ingredients, mixing until blended. Chill.

WARNING: dogs do eat asparagus

did someone say treat?

snow days are bestest days

Cold hands – or in this case, cold noses – means a warm heart. Snow is perfect weather to take the girls out for their daily walk, and its perfect weather for soup. Wild Rice and Smoked Sausage of Beef Chile with Green Onion Scones is an ideal meal combination when it's chilly outside. Warm up with hot soup!

dolce making snow angels with the last of the snow
artists should never be rushed!

MEXICAN HAM SOUP
a great soup to throw on the stovetop and let simmer

2 cans pinto beans
8 c chicken broth
2 c chopped onions
1½ c cubed smoked ham steak
2 tbsp. ground cumin
1 tbsp. chile powder
1 bag frozen corn kernels
½ c diced green chile (Hatch Chile if you have them)
3 bay leaves
5 garlic cloves, crushed
2 cans diced tomatoes
1 smoked chipotle chile in adobo sauce + 2 tbsp. sauce

Cheddar cheese, grated
Sour cream for garnish

Combine beans, broth and the next 8 ingredients in a large pot. Bring to a boil. Partially cover and reduce heat to medium-low. Simmer 2 hours. Stir in the tomatoes and chipotle chile, simmer another 30 minutes.

Discard bay leaves and ladle soup into bowls. Top with grated cheese and sour cream.

"we like to eat snow. it's just easier than ice cubes" – amore and dolce

"ahhhh.... contentment"
tiamo

BEEF CHILE AND BEER
use a stout or dark beer for the chile, an IPA for yourself

1½ tbsp. ground cumin
1 tbsp. ground coriander
5 lbs. ground chuck (lean)
2 tbsp. oil
2½ lbs. onions, chopped
1½ lbs. red bell peppers, chopped
1½ lbs. green bell peppers, chopped
     (make the spouse do the chopping!)
3 cloves garlic (or more), minced
2-3 large jalapeno chile with seeds, chopped
7 tbsp. chile powder
2 tbsp. canned chipotle chile in adobo sauce (or more), minced
2 – 28-oz. cans crushed tomatoes with added puree
2 – 15-oz. cans kidney beans
2 bottles dark beer

Sauté ground beef in heavy, large pot until no longer pink, breaking up with a spoon. Heat oil in large skillet. Add onions, all the bell peppers, garlic and jalapenos and sauté until they begin to soften.

Add mixture to pot with beef. Mix well. Stir in spices, chile powder and chipotle chile. Add crushed tomatoes, beans and beer.

Bring to a boil, stirring occasionally. Reduce heat and simmer for about 1 hour, stirring often. Season with salt and pepper.

Ladle chile into bowls. Serve with sour cream, chopped green onions and grated cheese.

Okay to prepare ahead and freeze.

"we like messy cooks, they spill lots of cheese on the floor" – the girls

POSOLE
you may substitute pork instead of the chicken and use red chile

2 lbs. posole (found in the freezer section)
2–3 lbs. boneless & skinless chicken breast, cubed
8 c chicken broth (low sodium)
2½ c yellow or white onions, chopped
4–5 garlic cloves, minced
2–3 c fresh, roasted, peeled green chile, chopped
4 tbsp. butter
1½ tsp. oregano

1 c cilantro, chopped - optional
salt and pepper to taste
2 limes, sliced in wedges
sour cream for garnish

Cook the posole in 4 quarts of water in a large pot until tender, about 2 to 3 hours. You may need to add water throughout the cooking time. The posole is done when it is soft and the kernels begin to burst, like popcorn. Drain and put back into the pot.

Melt the butter in a cast-iron skillet and sauté the chicken, onions and garlic until the chicken is cooked. Add chicken, onions and garlic to the pot of posole, along with the oregano, chile and chicken broth. Bring to a boil – reduce heat and simmer for about 30 minutes.

Season with salt and pepper and continue cooking for another 30 minutes. Add the cilantro.

Serve with lime wedges and a dollop of sour cream if desired.

"i guess this is human food" – the girls

FRENCH ONION SOUP

3 tbsp. butter
1 tbsp. olive oil
4 large yellow onions, thinly sliced
½ tsp. salt
½ tsp. sugar
3 tbsp. flour
2½ c beef broth (low sodium)
2½ c chicken broth (low sodium)
½ c water
½ c vermouth (or a bit more)

grated Swiss or Parmesan cheese
French bread rounds, toasted

In a cast-iron pot, melt butter and add olive oil and onion slices. Cover and cook slowly, about 25 minutes. Uncover and add salt and sugar. Continue cooking and stirring occasionally until golden brown – about 30 to 40 minutes. Sprinkle flour over onions and stir for several minutes.

Add broths, water and vermouth. Simmer partly covered for 40 minutes. Skim remaining oil from top.

Serve with toasted bread rounds and top with cheese of your choice.

"would you cook something we can eat?" – all the girls

amore – the snow is her domain

MALC'S MINESTRONE SOUP

1 c dried pink beans
½ lb. green beans
1 c dried split peas
1 tbsp. dried basil
1 c barley
1 tbsp. salt
12 c beef broth (low sodium)
½ tsp. pepper
3-4 garlic cloves, minced
2 zucchini, chopped
6 tomatoes, peeled and chopped
2 carrots, chopped
½ c fresh parsley, chopped
3 celery stalks, diced

2 tbsp. tomato paste
8 bacon slices, diced
2/3 c small macaroni pasta
3 onions, chopped
½ bunch chopped spinach
1 c celery, chopped
1 c frozen corn kernels
1 leek, minced
½ lb. Parmesan cheese, grated
2 c yellow summer squash, cut
  in bite-sized pieces
1 – 16-oz. can kidney bean
1 – 16-oz. can garbanzo beans

In a large pot, cover the split peas and pink beans with water and soak overnight. The next day, drain water, rinse and add barley, broth, garlic, tomatoes, parsley and tomato paste. Set aside.

In a small skillet, fry the bacon until crisp. Remove the bacon and set aside on paper towels to drain, reserving the bacon fat. Chop the bacon into small pieces. Using the reserved bacon fat, sauté the onions, celery, and leek over low heat until limp.

Remove the onion mixture and add to the bean and pea mixture. Add the bacon along with the basil, salt and pepper. Cover and set over low heat. Simmer for 2 hours. Add the squash, kidney beans, garbanzo beans, green beans, zucchini, carrots, celery, spinach and corn and continue to cook for another 45 minutes. Add the wine and pasta and cook for 3-4 more hours.

Ladle into large soup bowls and garnish with grated Parmesan cheese and toasted bread rounds.

"takes forever, but worth it!" - the husband

you better leave some for me

WILD RICE WITH SMOKED SAUSAGE

13 c chicken broth (low sodium)
1¼ c wild rice
6¼ c frozen corn kernels (about 2½ lbs.), thawed
2 tbsp. vegetable oil
1 lb. cooked Kielbasa sausage, cut into ½ inch cubes
3 carrots, peeled and diced
2 medium onions, chopped

1½ c half and half cream
1 c fresh parsley, chopped

Bring 5 cups of chicken broth to simmer in heavy medium saucepan. Add wild rice and simmer until all the liquid evaporates and rice is almost tender, about 45 minutes.

In a food processor, take 4 cups of the corn kernels and 1½ cups chicken broth and puree. Continue until smooth. You might need to do this in batches.

Heat oil in heavy, large cast-iron pan. Add sausage and sauté until brown, about 5 minutes. Add onions and carrots and cook another 3 minutes. Add remaining chicken broth and bring to a simmer. Simmer for another 20 minutes.

Add cooked wild rice, corn puree and rest of corn kernels. Continue cooking until rice is tender, about 30 minutes.

Soup can be prepared up to this point two days ahead. Refrigerate.
Reheat soup over medium heat. Once heated, add half and half.

Ladle into soup bowls. Sprinkle chopped parsley over top.

WARNING: do not turn your back on the sausage

BLEU CHEESE AND BACON SOUP
if you like bleu cheese, you'll love this!

2 c yellow onion, chopped
1 large leek (white and pale green parts only), chopped
3 celery stalks, chopped
2 medium carrots, peeled and chopped
4 c chicken broth (low sodium)
10 bacon slices, diced
1 large potato, peeled and cubed
1 c dry white wine
5 oz. crumbled bleu cheese
salt and pepper

Cook bacon in heavy, large skillet over medium heat until crispy. Transfer bacon to paper towels and drain. Crumble bacon and set aside. Keep wooden spoon close by to whack fingers and paws going after the bacon.

Save 2 tbsp. of bacon drippings and add onions, leek, celery and carrots. Cook until they begin to soften, about 15 minutes. In a large pot, add onions, leek, celery, carrots, broth, potato and wine. Bring to boil. Simmer until all vegetables are tender, about 30-40 minutes. Remove from heat.

Place bleu cheese in food processor. Add 1 cup hot soup. Blend until cheese melts and mixture is smooth. Return cheese mixture to soup in large pot and stir to blend.

Season with salt and pepper to taste. Ladle soup into bowls. Sprinkle with bacon crumbles and serve.

"we like bleu cheese" – the girls

PEACH AND AMARETTO SOUP
serve cold as a first course

1½ lbs. peaches, peeled, pitted and sliced
2 c sour cream or plain low-fat yogurt
1 c fresh orange juice with pulp
1 c pineapple juice
½ c amaretto
2 tbsp. fresh lemon juice
brown sugar to taste

raspberries
mint leaves
orange zest

Puree peaches in food processor until smooth. Add sour cream, orange juice, pineapple juice, amaretto and lemon juice. Blend well. You might need to blend contents in batches. Add brown sugar to sweeten to taste. Chill.

Serve in fun clear glasses and garnish with raspberries, orange zest and mint leaves.

"woooo, weeee, georgia peaches!" – dolce

canned peaches ... a favorite!

bread & dog biscuits

I learned the hard way to hide the Pumpkin Bread from the girls and my husband. Enough said!

dog bones are great puppy-sitters,
but only under adult supervision

GOAT CHEESE AND GREEN ONION SCONES

2 c all-purpose flour
1 tbsp. baking powder
1 tsp. salt
½ tsp. ground pepper
4 oz. chilled soft mild goat cheese (such as Montrachet)
3 large green onions, thinly chopped
¼ c half and half cream
1 large egg
½ c Parmesan cheese, shredded

Preheat oven to 375°F. Mix first 4 ingredients together in a large bowl. Add cheese and green onions and toss with a fork. Beat cream and egg in small bowl. Stir egg mixture into dry ingredients and mix gently until dough forms. Divide dough in half. On a lightly floured surface, flatten each piece into 1" thick rounds. Transfer rounds to baking sheet, spacing evenly between rounds. Cut each round into 6 wedges. Sprinkle Parmesan cheese over top of each round. Bake scones until tops are golden brown – about 25 minutes. Cool 10 minutes and serve warm. Makes 12 scones.

Delicious with butter or try with mustard and ham. Also goes well with chile.

"we prefer just good ol' dog biscuits!" – amore and dolce

CORNBREAD BISCUITS WITH CHILE AND CHEDDAR

1 tbsp. unsalted butter
¾ c green onions, chopped (packed)
1½ c all-purpose flour
1 tbsp. sugar
2½ tsp. baking powder
¾ tsp. coarse kosher salt
½ tsp. baking soda
1 stick (½ c) unsalted butter, cut into small cubes
1½ c sharp Cheddar cheese, grated
1 large egg
¾ c buttermilk
1 tbsp. canned chipotle chile in adobo sauce, finely minced
1 egg, beaten + 1 tbsp. whipping cream for glaze

Preheat oven to 425°F. Melt 1 tbsp. butter in skillet over medium heat and add green onions until softened. Remove from heat.

Using a food processor, blend flour, cornmeal, sugar, baking powder, salt and baking soda. Add ½ cup chilled butter. Using the pulse button, mix until it resembles coarse meal. Add cheese and pulse until mixed. Transfer flour mixture to a large bowl.

Whisk 1 egg in glass measuring cup. Add enough buttermilk to egg to measure 1 cup. Stir in green onion and chipotles. Make a well in center of the flour ingredients and pour buttermilk mixture into the well. Mix just until evenly blended. Don't over mix.

Turn dough out onto floured surface. Knead gently until dough holds together. Pat out on surface to about ¾ inch to 1 inch thick. Cut out biscuits with cutter, transfer to ungreased baking sheet and brush with egg glaze. Bake biscuits until golden brown – about 18 minutes. Serve warm.

"we can't eat onions, distract us with some dog biscuits instead – we'll catch them!" – the girls

WARNING: adorable puppies make caregivers
buy every dog toy at the pet store

amore

PUMPKIN SPICE BREAD

do not leave on the counter - dogs and husbands can't be trusted

1¼ c all-purpose flour
¾ c quick oats
2 tsp. baking soda
1½ tsp. pumpkin pie spice
½ tsp. baking powder
½ tsp. salt
2 tsp. cinnamon
1 tsp. nutmeg
3 eggs
1¾ c solid pack pumpkin (16-oz. can)
3 c brown sugar
½ c water
½ c canola oil
½ c evaporated milk
1 c pinon nuts, coarsely chopped

Combine the first 8 ingredients in a large bowl. Beat eggs, pumpkin, brown sugar, water, oil and evaporated milk in large mixer bowl on medium speed until all combined. Mix flour mixture into pumpkin mixture on low speed until blended. Stir in pinon nuts. Spoon into 2 greased loaf pans.

Bake in a preheated 350°F oven for 60-70 minutes or until wooden pick inserted in center comes out clean. Cool for 10 minutes and remove from pans.

"now this is heaven!" – amore and dolce

WARNING: leaving bread to cool on the counter is NOT an option with amore and dolce in the house - these two thieves ate a whole loaf in two gulps!

"pummmkin is one of our very, very favorites" – amore and dolce

SWEET CINNAMON BISCUITS

2 c sifted all-purpose flour
1 tbsp. baking powder
1 tsp. salt
¼ tsp. baking soda
¼ c canola oil
¾ c low-fat buttermilk
1 stick (½ c) butter, softened
¾ c brown sugar
1 tsp. cinnamon

Combine flour, baking powder, salt and baking soda in a medium bowl and mix well. Stir in canola oil. Add buttermilk and stir until just blended.

Knead the dough on a lightly floured surface until smooth. Roll dough into a 15 inch x 8 inch rectangle.

Preheat the oven to 400°F. Lightly grease a 9-inch round baking pan. Spread butter over the dough. Combine brown sugar and cinnamon in a small bowl. Sprinkle over butter.

Roll up rectangle, jellyroll fashion, starting from one long side. Pinch seam to seal.

Cut the roll into 1½-inch slices. Arrange in prepared baking pan. Bake until lightly browned, about 15-18 minutes. Remove from oven, count the number of biscuits (just in case there is a thief) and serve hot.

"yummmm" – tiamo

could anything be sweeter?

GARLICKY CHEESY BREAD
an ooey gooey treat

¼ stick butter, softened
2 tbsp. mayonnaise
3 garlic cloves, smushed
1 1/3 c feta cheese, crumbled
1¼ c Parmesan cheese, grated and divided
¾ c Monterey Jack cheese, grated and packed
½ c green onions, finely chopped
12 thick slices (¾-inch-thick) farm bread or ciabatta bread

Position the oven rack in the center of oven and preheat to 475°F.

Mix the first 3 ingredients in medium bowl. Mix in feta, ½ c Parmesan, Monterey Jack cheese and onions.

Spread 2 tbsp. cheese mixture onto each bread slice. Sprinkle Parmesan on top of each bread slice. Press Parmesan to adhere.

Place on baking sheet. Sprinkle lightly with salt and pepper. Bake until cheese is golden brown and bubbly, about 10-12 minutes.

"once again, something we can't have" – the disappointed trio

48

we'll growl over the tiniest crumb ... or shoe

always have dessert first so there's enough room

I've never understood why the dessert section is always placed at the back of a cookbook. It's the best part of any meal and extra room in the tummy should always be saved for sweet concoctions. I purposely moved this section up a few notches in the cookbook, knowing the old cliché "save the best for last" does not apply to dessert!

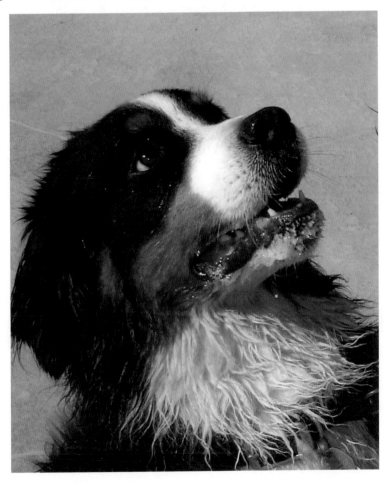

tiamo after playing in the paw pool

HOMEMADE GEORGIA PEACH ICE CREAM

3 lbs. fresh peaches, peeled, pitted and chopped
½ c brown sugar
1 pint heavy cream
2 - 14-oz. cans sweetened condensed milk
2 tsp. Kahlua (or more)
2 c whole milk

Puree peaches, sugar and cream in blender or food processor.

In a gallon ice cream freezer container, mix together the peach mixture, sweetened condensed milk and Kahlua. Pour in enough whole milk to fill the container to the fill line.

Follow the manufacturer's instructions to freeze the ice cream.

"ohhh babeee, ohh babeee, oh babeee! more peaches" – tiamo, amore and dolce

BISCOCHITOS – A New Mexico tradition

If you add too much brandy, you might end up naming these morsels the "bitch-cookies"

6 c flour
1½ c sugar
2 c pure lard (ick! but necessary)
2 eggs
1 tsp. baking powder
1 tsp. salt
12 tsp. anise seeds
½ c brandy
A couple sips of brandy for the cook
½ c sugar and 1 tbsp. cinnamon mixed together and set aside

Cream lard and sugar well. Add eggs one at a time, then add the anise seeds and mix well. Sift dry ingredients and blend with lard/sugar mixture. Add brandy.

Roll out on a floured board. Cut into shapes and sprinkle with the sugar and cinnamon mixture.

Bake in a preheated oven at 350°F for 10 to 12 minutes until golden brown.

This recipe was given to me by Eva Maestas, a true New Mexican who is also a good friend and special co-worker. She'll know if you try to sneak Crisco shortening instead of lard into the recipe!

"WOW! A cookie named after us" – the proud trio

HONEY GLAZED GRILLED PINEAPPLE

½ c honey
¼ c fresh lime juice
1 tbsp. lime peel, grated
1 tsp. orange flower water (sold at liquor stores, but not a deal-breaker if you can't find)
1 large ripe pineapple
¼ c fresh mint, minced

Whisk the first 4 ingredients in a large glass baking dish.

Remove the rind from the pineapple and cut crosswise into 6 rounds. Remove core (it should look like a donut). Add pineapple to dish, turning to coat. Cover and let stand at room temperature at least 1 to 2 hours.

Prepare grill to medium heat. Remove pineapple from marinade, reserving the rest of the marinade. Grill until golden brown, about 3 minutes each side.

Transfer to serving dish. Pour saved marinade over the pineapple slices. Sprinkle with mint. Serve warm or chilled.

"pineapple is not one of our favorites, but we'll still gulp it down" – tiamo, amore and dolce

PUFFED PEAR PACKAGES STUFFED WITH CHOCOLATE
a fancy-dancy dessert with a "WOW" factor

6 medium ripe pears (Anjou)
1 – 6-oz. package dark chocolate chips
1 egg
1 tbsp. water
1 package frozen puff pastry sheets, thawed
flour
1 jar caramel sauce, heated
mint leaves for garnish

Carefully peel pears, leaving stems intact. Cut pears in half just above the thickest part of the pear. Scoop out core using small spoon or melon ball scooper. DO NOT break through the sides or bottom of pear. Place chocolate chips in scooped out cavity. Put pear top back on. Rub with lemon juice to avoid browning.

Roll out pastry sheet to a 10-inch x 13-inch rectangle on a lightly floured surface. Cut 6 squares – about 3½ inches x 3½ inches. Set remaining pastry aside.

Beat egg and water together and set aside.

Set a pear in the middle of each pastry square and bring the 4 corners together at the top of the pear, letting the stem peek out. Pinch the seams together. Brush with egg mixture. Pears may be prepared 1 day ahead.

Set pears on ungreased baking sheet and bake 15 minutes in a preheated oven at 425°F. Reduce heat to 375°F and bake an additional 7-8 minutes longer until pastry is golden brown.

Place pear on dessert plate and drizzle hot caramel sauce over each pear. Garnish with a mint leaf. Serve immediately.

"we have decided we like pears and caramel sauce" – dolce and tiamo

FRUIT COBBLER

Pick a fruit, any fruit (except a citrus) – apples, plums, berries, peaches, apricots or a combo of your favorites

8 c of your favorite fruit – fresh or frozen
1 c brown sugar
½ c instant tapioca
juice from a lime
½ tsp. salt

Preheat oven to 375°F. Toss fruit with sugar, tapioca, lime juice and salt in a bowl. Place in a shallow 2-quart glass baking dish. Set aside.

1 c all-purpose flour
¾ c brown sugar
½ c chopped nuts (your choice)
½ tsp. baking powder
½ tsp. salt
1 stick (½ c) cold unsalted butter, cut into small cubes
1 egg

Mix together the first 5 ingredients. Mix in the butter cubes, using your fingers until the mixture is coarse in texture. Blend in the egg.

Spread the flour mixture in clumps over the fruit, covering evenly.

Bake for 45 to 50 minutes until golden brown. Cool for an hour before serving, allowing the juices to thicken.

Serve with vanilla ice cream.

"sniff, sniff – something smells good!" – tiamo, amore and dolce

a perfect summer treat after playing at the paw pool!

Dolce...

The "dolch". Dolce was one of the smaller pups in the litter, and, from day one, she was determined to be next to me or on me. When we took the puppies to the vet for their first set of shots, she somehow ended up on my lap. From then on, she has been our 100-pound lap dog.

When she was 6 months old, she needed surgery on both shoulders. While recovering, Dolce would sit on the sidelines with Malcolm and me, watching Tiamo and Amore play. This turned her into a big cuddle bug. Boy, does she love her hugs!

Of the three, Dolce is the most passive, except when it comes to loading up into the car. She could be 20 yards behind the other two, but it's a sure bet she'll be in the car and on my lap before either Tiamo or Amore can even think about jumping up into the car. It's a sight for other drivers when they pass us.

Today, Dolce is one of the sweetest dogs. She still wants to be right next to me. She still comes up on the bed for a night-time cuddle session. She still wants the front seat of the car (passenger beware). And, she still climbs onto my lap no matter where we are.

Dolce has lived up to her name.

dolce – our sweet brat!

pummkins, yoogurt & bannannas
three of our most favorite things

BAKED BANANAS

2 bananas
1 lime (squeezed for juice)
2 tbsp. dark rum
½ tsp. ground cinnamon
1/8 tsp. ground nutmeg
2 tbsp. dark brown sugar
2 tbsp. butter

Preheat oven to 400°F. Peel the bananas and slice in half lengthwise. Lay the pieces into a buttered 9 inch x 13 inch glass ovenproof dish. Pour the lime juice and rum evenly over the bananas. Sprinkle the spices and sugar over the bananas. Dot with butter. Keep out of reach from dogs.

Bake for 10-15 minutes. Serve hot, topped with vanilla ice cream.

"we'll sit really good, we promise, for a slice of bannanna!" – amore and dolce

the guilty culprits

DUSTED STRAWBERRIES and YOGURT

½ c sugar
½ tsp. ground cardamom
¼ c Grand Marnier or other orange liqueur
2 – 16-oz. baskets of strawberries, hulled and left whole
1 container vanilla yogurt

Whisk sugar and cardamom in small bowl to blend.

Pour Grand Marnier into large bowl. Add strawberries and toss to coat. Spread sugar mixture on a baking sheet. Working in batches, transfer strawberries to baking sheet and roll to coat strawberries in sugar mixture.

Divide strawberries into 6 wine, martini or margarita glasses. Pour any leftover Grand Marnier from the bowl over the berries. Cover and chill. Serve with yogurt.

"any fruit, we'll swallow, except oranges; those aren't so tasty" - the girls

PUMPKIN PANCAKES

2 c Bisquick mix
2 tbsp. brown sugar
2 tsp. cinnamon
1 tsp. allspice
2 eggs

1 tsp. vanilla
1 – 12-oz. can evaporated milk
½ c solid packed canned pumpkin
2 tbsp. oil

In a large mixing bowl, combine all the above ingredients and mix well. Lightly grease a nonstick griddle and heat to medium. Pour ¼ to ½ cup pancake mix onto griddle for each pancake.

Cook until top surface is bubbly and edges are lightly browned. Flip and cook other side the same. Remove from griddle and serve with warm maple syrup.

"our favorite!" – tiamo, amore and dolce

a quick nibble...

COOKIE CUP BASKETS

when you want to impress, this makes a great presentation

¼ lb. butter
¼ c brown sugar
¼ c light corn syrup
3½ tbsp. all-purpose flour
½ c finely chopped almonds
1 tsp. vanilla

In a 2-quart pan, melt butter over low heat, add brown sugar and syrup. Cook over high heat, stirring until liquid boils. Remove from heat and blend in flour and nuts. Stir in vanilla.

Grease and flour a 12 inch x 15 inch baking sheet. For each cookie, place 2-3 tbsp. of the batter 8 inches apart on the baking sheet. Bake at 325°F for about 12 minutes. Take out of oven and cool for 1 minute.

When cookie edges are firm enough to lift, loosen with spatula and remove carefully – they should be hot and malleable. Drape over an upended glass that is at least 2 inches wide at the bottom to mold into a cup. Keep the bottom of cookie flat but the sides may flare out. Cookie should firm into the shape within 2 minutes. Repeat the process with the rest of the cookie batter.

May be made ahead – store in an airtight container in a cool area. Serve with a small scoop of ice cream and top with your favorite fruit. Makes 4-6 cookie cups.

"any crumbs?" – tiamo counter-surfing during a drive-by in the kitchen

who needs a cookie when you can have a shoe?

CHOCOLATE SIN

1 lb. sweet chocolate pieces
6 oz. (1½ sticks unsalted) butter
4 eggs
1 tbsp. sugar
1 tbsp. flour

8 oz. raspberries
superfine sugar
1 c heavy cream
1 tbsp. amaretto
fresh raspberries

Preheat oven to 400°F. Line an 8-inch cake pan with parchment paper. Set aside.

Place uncracked eggs in hot tap water for 5 minutes to take the chill off. Melt chocolate and butter over low heat in a saucepan. Crack the eggs and mix with sugar with an electric mixer. Beat on high speed for 10 minutes or until it has tripled in size. Sift the flour on top. Fold into the egg mixture. Stir a little bit of the egg mixture into the chocolate. Carefully fold the remaining egg mixture into the chocolate until completely blended.

Pour into the prepared pan. Bake for 20 minutes. The middle of cake should be slightly soft. Cool completely. Cover and refrigerate in the pan overnight. May be frozen for two weeks.

Puree the 8 oz. of raspberries and strain. Add enough superfine sugar to sweeten to taste. Beat the heavy cream with the amaretto and sugar to sweeten until peaks are firm.

Invert the cake onto a serving platter. Drizzle the raspberry puree over the top and add the fresh raspberries and whipped cream.

ABSOLUTELY NEVER GIVE CHOCOLATE TO YOUR DOG!

sigh, i don't get to eat chocolate (with a pout thrown in)

ELDORADO COOKIES

WARNING: cookies have disappeared from rack due to four-legged thieves

1 c butter
1 c brown sugar
1 c white sugar
1 tsp. vanilla
½ tsp. salt
2 eggs
2 c flour
2 tsp. baking soda
1 tsp. baking powder
1 c oatmeal
1 c coconut
2 c corn flakes
1 c chocolate chips

Cream together butter and sugars until all the butter lumps are smooth. Set aside.

Cream together vanilla, salt and eggs. Add to the butter mixture. Set aside.

Sift together flour, baking soda, and baking powder and add to the butter/eggs mixture until completely blended. Add the remaining ingredients and mix.

Bake in a preheated oven at 350°F on greased baking sheets for 12 to 15 minutes.

Cool on cookie racks. Hide.

"not even a crumb?" – the trio

"dang! we didn't eat that much!"

RED VELVET CAKE
it's the best! (seriously, this is better than anything you could buy)

2½ c sifted cake flour
½ c cocoa powder
1 tsp. baking soda
1 tsp. baking powder
1 tsp. salt
2 c sugar
1 c unsalted butter, softened (2 sticks)
4 eggs
1 c sour cream
1 c buttermilk
1 c canola oil
2 oz. red food coloring
1 tsp. distilled white vinegar
2 tsp. vanilla extract

FROSTING

2 – 8-oz. pkg. cream cheese, softened
1 c unsalted butter, softened
1-lb. box confectioners' sugar
1 tsp. vanilla extract

Preheat the oven to 350°F. Grease and flour two 9-inch cake pans. Sift together flour, cocoa, baking soda, baking powder and salt. Set aside. Cream together sugar and butter. Beat in eggs, one at a time. Alternately, add flour mixture and buttermilk, oil and sour cream. Beat in food coloring and vinegar, then add vanilla. Spread batter evenly in the greased pans.

Bake for 20-30 minutes or until a wooden toothpick inserted into the center comes out clean. Turn out onto a rack to cool.

In large bowl, combine the cream cheese and butter. Beat in confectioners' sugar until fluffy. Beat in vanilla. Frost cake.

WARNING: watch husband. Unsupervised, he will take just a little taste, until gone!

BEST EVER CARROT CAKE YOU'LL EVER MAKE
no lie! it's that good!

2 c cake flour
2 tsp. baking soda
2 tsp. baking powder
½ tsp. salt
2 tsp. ground cinnamon
3 large eggs
2 c brown sugar
¾ c canola oil
¾ c buttermilk
2 tsp. vanilla extract

2 c carrot, grated
1 – 8-oz. can crushed pineapple
1 c golden raisins
½ c applesauce
1 – 3½-oz. can flaked coconut
1 tsp. coconut extract
1 c chopped pecans

FROSTING

4 c confectioners' sugar
2 tsp. vanilla extract

2 – 8-oz. pkg. cream cheese
4 tbsp. butter, softened

Preheat oven at 350°F. Line three 9-inch round cake pans with parchment paper. Lightly grease and flour paper. Set aside.

Stir together first 5 ingredients. Set aside.

Beat together eggs and sugar until smooth. Add oil, buttermilk and vanilla. Add flour mixture, beating at a low speed until blended. Fold in the remaining ingredients.

Bake for 25-30 minutes or until a wooden toothpick inserted in the center comes out clean. Cool in pans on wire racks.

Cream together the confectioners' sugar, cream cheese, vanilla and butter until smooth. Frost cake and lock up.

WARNING: you'll need to hide this from husbands and dogs, otherwise, claiming the need for beta-carotene, they will eat it all!

LEMON NAPOLEONS

½ c superfine sugar
2 large eggs
2 large egg yolks
½ c fresh lemon juice, strained
6 tbsp. unsalted butter
2 tsp. lemon peel, grated
8 tbsp. sugar

2 tsp. ground cinnamon
6 sheets phyllo pastry, thawed
6 tbsp. unsalted butter, melted
1 c chilled heavy cream
2 tsp. sugar
1 tsp. vanilla extract

Whisk sugar, eggs and yolks in a heavy medium saucepan until blended. Mix in lemon juice, butter and lemon peel. Whisk over medium-low heat until mixture thickens and is just starting to bubble at the edges, approximately 6 minutes.

DO NOT BOIL. Transfer to a small bowl and press plastic wrap directly onto surface of curd to avoid crusting. Chill until cold. May be made 3 days ahead. Keep chilled.

Position one rack in bottom third and the other rack in center of oven. Preheat oven to 375°F. Line 2 baking sheets with parchment paper.

Mix sugar and cinnamon in a small bowl. Place 1 phyllo sheet on work surface. Until ready to use, cover remaining phyllo with plastic wrap and a damp cloth. Brush phyllo with melted butter and sprinkle with 1 tsp. cinnamon sugar. Top with second sheet of phyllo and brush with butter and sprinkle with cinnamon sugar. Repeat layering with remaining 4 sheets of phyllo. Cut phyllo stack into four 3-inch x 18-inch strips. Cut each strip into six 3-inch squares, making 24 squares. Transfer to baking sheets. Bake phyllo squares 8 minutes.

Beat heavy cream, 2 tbsp. butter and vanilla until stiff peaks form. Arrange 8 pastries on work surface. Spoon lemon curd onto each pastry. Top with second pastry square. Spoon whipped cream on pastry layer and top with third pastry.

Lightly dust napoleons with powdered sugar and serve.

"we once tried to eat a lemon wedge – uck!" – the girls

we are not begging, just hyper-vigilant about the possibility
of food dropping from heaven.

CRÈME DE MENTHE GRAPES

1 lb. seedless grapes, washed and dried
½ c crème de menthe
½ c confectioner's sugar

Separate grapes into small clusters. Dip each cluster into crème de menthe and dust generously with sugar. Place on a foil-lined baking sheet and freeze for 30 minutes. When ready to serve, arrange grapes on tray and sprinkle again lightly with confectioners' sugar.

May serve a top on a Brie wheel as a garnish or by itself.

"DO NOT FEED US GRAPES!" – the girls

AMARETTO SAUCE

8 oz. ricotta cheese
1 – 8-oz. pkg. cream cheese, softened
½ c brown sugar
4 egg yolks
2 tbsp. heavy cream
3 tbsp. amaretto
fresh fruit such as kiwis, bananas, apples, grapes, pineapple, peaches, cantaloupes, strawberries, blackberries or honeydew melon

Using food processor, mix together the ricotta cheese and cream cheese until smooth. Add sugar, egg yolks, heavy cream and amaretto. Keep beating until smooth. Pour into a 3-cup serving bowl. Chill until ready to serve. Arrange fresh fruit around the sauce on a serving platter.

Garnish with mint leaves.

one of our little munchkins

yes, we eat lettuce too

and grass and rocks and sticks and dirt and paper and...

Many times, salads are the first hint of what's to come. Throw away the token cucumber and radish slice often served with a 60's-style salad. Here are some salad treats that are different, unique and delicious! Like children, dogs put anything in their mouth. I was amazed when I first saw Dolce eat some dropped lettuce and tomato. These delicious first course meals will be a tantalizing clue to the next dish.

a tired dog is a VERY happy owner

STUFFED TOMATOES WITH SHRIMP SALAD

1 lb. bay shrimp, peeled and cooked
1 stalk celery, finely chopped
½ c fresh basil, minced
10 kalamata olives, pitted and chopped
1 medium shallot, minced
2 tbsp. low-fat sour cream
1 tbsp. white wine vinegar
salt and pepper to taste
4 large ripe tomatoes, cored and hollowed out

Combine shrimp, celery, basil, olives shallot, sour cream, vinegar, salt and pepper in a medium bowl. Stir to combine.

Fill each tomato with a generous ½ cup of shrimp salad. Sprinkle with a ½ tsp. of dried dill.

May also use on a hoagie roll for a shrimp salad sandwich.

"don't give us shrimp peels; they're bad for our throats" - tiamo, amore and dolce

THE WEDGE
simple but elegant

¾ c nonfat sour cream
¾ c mayonnaise (may substitute with plain yogurt)
2 tbsp. fresh lemon juice
1 tbsp. coarsely ground black pepper
5 drops hot pepper sauce (or more!)
1 c bleu cheese crumbles
nonfat buttermilk to thin

¾ lb. bacon, thick cut, cut into 1-inch pieces
1 large head iceberg lettuce
1 large red onion, sliced in thin rings

Place salad plates in freezer to chill several hours before plating.

Mix sour cream, mayonnaise, lemon juice, ground pepper and hot pepper sauce together. Add bleu cheese crumbles. Stir until well blended. Add a little buttermilk if too thick. Refrigerate until ready to use.

Cook bacon in large cast-iron skillet until crispy; drain and set aside. Core the head of iceberg lettuce and cut into 4 to 6 wedges depending on the lettuce head size. Arrange lettuce wedges on chilled plates. Drizzle dressing over lettuce wedge. Sprinkle bacon on top and garnish with red onion rings. Serve chilled.

"we love bleu cheese!" – the girls

MY BIG FAT GREEK WEDDING SALAD

this is a great salad for large crowds

¼ c + 1 tbsp. olive oil
¼ c red wine vinegar
½ tsp. dried oregano
½ tsp. salt
½ tsp. pepper

2 romaine lettuce heads, rinsed and dried
3 large tomatoes, cut up in wedges
1 cucumber, sliced
1 yellow bell pepper, chopped
1 red onion, chopped
½ c pitted kalamata olives
¾ c feta cheese crumbles

Prepare the first 5 ingredients for the dressing. Whisk until blended. Refrigerate until ready to use.

Tear the greens into pieces. Place in a large salad bowl and add the tomatoes, cucumber, bell pepper, onion and olives.

Toss with dressing until coated and top with feta cheese crumbles just before serving.

"we just want a big fat treat!" – tiamo, amore and dolce

yes, we chew anything, everything and all things

FAUX CAESAR SALAD

½ c olive oil
2 tbsp. red wine vinegar
2 tbsp. fresh lemon juice
1 tbsp. Worcestershire sauce
1 tsp. Dijon mustard
1 tsp. lemon peel, grated
4-5 garlic cloves, minced
5-8 drops Tabasco sauce
2 large heads romaine lettuce, torn into pieces
2/3 c fresh Parmesan cheese, grated
freshly ground pepper to taste

homemade croutons (see recipe below)

Whisk together the first 8 ingredients. Refrigerate until ready to use. Add lettuce to a large salad bowl and add croutons (as many as desired), Parmesan cheese and pepper. Add dressing and toss until dressing has coated the lettuce. Serve chilled. Sprinkle a little extra Parmesan cheese over the top just before serving.

HOMEMADE CROUTONS

3 bagels (onion or garlic), cut into ¼-inch rounds.
1½ tbsp. olive oil or butter
3 - 4 large garlic cloves, minced
3 tbsp. butter

Preheat oven to 325°F. Combine olive oil, garlic and butter in a saucepan and heat until butter has melted. Set aside. Place sliced bagels on a baking sheet. Brush with oil mixture. Bake until crisp and brown, about 30 minutes. Cool and store in an airtight container at room temperature. May be used with soup as well.

(husband strongly disagrees with idea of croutons... "it's just crummy stale bread and a waste of calories!")

amore's first adventure in the big world

COMMON GARDEN VARIETIES

SLICED TOMATO SALAD
a great colorful salad and easy too!

4 beefsteak tomatoes, sliced
feta cheese crumbles
pesto (see recipe on page 13)
salt and pepper

In the middle of a serving platter, place a small bowl. Fill bowl with pesto. Arrange tomato slices on platter circling the pesto bowl. Sprinkle with salt and pepper to taste. Sprinkle with feta cheese crumbles. Chill until ready to serve.

HEIRLOOM TOMATO SALAD WITH HERBS AND CAPERS

2 c heirloom cherry tomatoes, halved
2 lbs. assorted heirloom beefsteak tomatoes, cut into wedges
    mix up the variety for color and taste
½ c feta cheese crumbles
¼ c basil, thinly sliced
3 tbsp. fresh parsley, chopped
2 tbsp. fresh mint, chopped
1 tbsp. drained capers
3 tbsp. balsamic vinegar
3 tbsp. olive oil
1 tsp. salt and pepper

1 sourdough bread loaf, cut into slices

Combine first 9 ingredients in a bowl. Sprinkle with salt and pepper. Toss gently. Set aside. Grill or toast sourdough bread slices. Serve 1¼ cup tomato mixture with one bread slice.

"tomatoes aren't too bad!" - tiamo

tiamo, our momma

THE SPINACH DUEL

HOT SPINACH SALAD
the red pepper jelly adds a snap and a pop to the dressing

¼ c red pepper jelly
2 tbsp. cider vinegar
1 tbsp. olive oil
½ tsp. salt and pepper
8 c fresh spinach
1 small red onion, thinly sliced
½ c Gorgonzola cheese crumbles
½ c roasted pistachio nuts

Microwave red pepper jelly in a glass measuring cup for 30 seconds. Add vinegar, oil, salt and pepper. Set aside to cool.

Mix spinach, red onion slices and Gorgonzola cheese crumbles in a large salad bowl. Drizzle dressing over spinach and toss well. Sprinkle with nuts and serve.

RASPBERRY SPINACH SALAD
a great summer salad for the ladies

10 c fresh spinach, rinsed and dried
1 c fresh raspberries
1 c macadamia nuts
3 kiwi fruit, peeled and sliced

4 tbsp. raspberry vinegar
4 tbsp. raspberry jam
1 c olive oil

Combine spinach with raspberries, kiwis and nuts. Set aside. Whisk together vinegar, jam and oil. Drizzle dressing over spinach mixture and toss until coated. Top the salad with additional nuts and raspberries.

"we love raspberries!" – amore and dolce

a very pregnant momma

MY FAVORITE TORTELLINI SALAD

12 oz. frozen tortellini pasta
3 tbsp. red wine vinegar
1 tsp. dried basil
2 tsp. Dijon mustard
1 tsp. each salt and pepper
3 garlic cloves, minced
½ c olive oil
¼ c. fresh parsley, finely chopped
3 oz. dry salami, thinly sliced
1 red bell pepper, thinly sliced in strips
1 red onion, chopped
¼ c green onions, chopped
2 tbsp. toasted pine nuts
4 tbsp. Parmesan cheese, grated

1 head butter lettuce

Cook pasta according to directions. Rinse with cold water and drain. Set aside.

Mix vinegar, basil, mustard, salt, pepper and garlic in a large bowl. Add oil until well blended.

Gently mix together tortellini, parsley, salami, bell pepper, red and green onions, pine nuts and Parmesan cheese. Blend in dressing. Cover and refrigerate.

Serve on lettuce leaves.

"make something i can eat.... pleeease!" - tiamo

being a puppy is hard work

HOT OFF THE GRILL PITA SALAD

2 tsp. garlic, minced
1 tsp. olive oil
4 pita rounds (6 inches)
1 tsp. salt and pepper
6 oz. Portobello mushrooms
1 white onion, sliced
2 medium tomatoes, sliced in ¼-inch slices
1/3 c spreadable goat cheese
½ c fresh basil, chopped

Preheat grill.

Combine garlic and oil and brush evenly over pita rounds. Sprinkle with half of the salt and pepper. Place pitas on grill and cook for 2 minutes on each side.

Sprinkle the remaining salt and pepper evenly over the mushrooms and tomatoes. Place mushrooms on grill and cook for 6 minutes or until tender. Grill onions until soft. Place tomatoes on grill and cook for one minute. If tomatoes are ripe, skip grilling them.

Spread goat cheese evenly over pitas. Top with mushrooms and then tomatoes. Sprinkle with the chopped basil.

Serve while still hot from the grill.

"come on... just a little bite" - dolce

deciding what to have for dinner

Amore...

Amore was, and still is, our "first-at-everything" puppy. She was the first pup to arrive in the world, the first to crawl, the first to climb out of the whelping pen, the first to bark, the first to jump and the first to start mischief!

Amore loves to run, just for the joy of running. Full of high-energy, she has three speeds: 1) idling with the engine revving, tail a-wagging, anxiously waiting for something to happen; 2) tail in the air, speeding through life; and 3) crashing into a fast sleep. Why walk when you can run through the house, land on a rug and get a free ride into the living room? Weeeeeee, look at meeeeeeeeee! CRASH! Yes, our living room has a bit of the trendy "lived-in" look.

She loves the snow and making snow angels, biting at the snow as she rolls over. She loves to ride in the car, head hanging out the window. When Malcolm parks the car and gets out for the store, she explodes and jumps into the driver's seat, ready for a fast get-away. There, she waits impatiently, on full alert for Malcolm to return. And, best of all, she loves to play chase with Malcolm; well, I should say, she really loves Malcolm chasing after her. Simply said, Amore loves life!

With shiny, bright eyes, Amore greets the morning before sunrise, ready to run through the day at full speed. We kept our little "first." Ahhh, a handful, yes, but such a joy in our lives.

"i'm going to enrich your life and drive you nuts"
amore peeking over the whelping pen

for the mature tongue
and those who will eat anything

Tiamo, Amore and Dolce are not picky eaters. Unlike children, they will eat anything. This section captures the tastes of a mature diner. Recipes with a twist, sauces with a kick and food with oomph, these entrees are easy to make and oh-so-good!

our mature queen

CHICKEN PICCATA

4 boneless, skinless chicken breasts, cut in half horizontally
flour for chicken breasts
2 tbsp. olive oil
4 garlic cloves, minced
½ glass dry white wine
1 c chicken broth
1 tbsp. capers
juice from ½ of lemon
¼ c parsley, chopped
1 glass dry white wine for the cook

Pound each half of chicken breast to a thinness of ½-inch thick. Lightly flour the chicken. Sauté in olive oil for about 1-2 minutes or until just golden on each side. Remove to a plate and set aside.

Toss garlic cloves into the same pan and lightly sauté. Pour in ½ glass of wine. Cook over high heat until it has reduced to a few spoonfuls. Add chicken broth and cook over high heat until reduced by half. Add capers, lemon juice and the chicken breasts. Sauté until warmed completely through. Place on a serving platter and sprinkle with parsley.

Serve with rice and asparagus.

WARNING: do not get up from the dinner table if dogs are under the table. Chicken gone.

BAYOU SHRIMP

great with fresh sourdough bread and some wine, of course!

¼ c unsalted butter
¼ c water
2 tbsp. fresh lemon juice
2 tsp. freshly ground black pepper
1½ tsp. fresh rosemary
1 tsp. paprika
1 tsp. Worcestershire sauce
12 uncooked large shrimp (in shells)

Melt butter in heavy medium saucepan over medium heat. Mix in water, lemon juice, pepper, rosemary, paprika and Worcestershire sauce.

Simmer sauce until reduced to ½ cup, about 3 minutes. Add shrimp and sprinkle with salt. Cover pan and cook until shrimp turns pink and are just cooked through, about 3 minutes. DO NOT OVER COOK.

Peel the shrimp at the table as you eat. Serves two.

"just smell that tantalizing aroma!" - tiamo

POLENTA PEPPER SOUFFLÉS

4 large red bell peppers
3 tbsp. butter
2 Anaheim chiles, seeded and minced
1 leek, sliced and diced
1 tsp. oregano
1 tsp. basil
¼ c polenta (coarsely ground cornmeal)
¾ c heavy cream
½ c shredded Monterey Jack cheese
3 egg yolks + 4 egg whites

Slice off tops of bell peppers. Finely chop the tops, and then hollow out peppers (discard core and seeds).

In heavy skillet, melt butter and sauté chopped bell pepper tops, chiles and sliced leeks until tender.

Add oregano, basil and polenta; cook for 1 minute. Add cream and stir. Bring mixture to a boil and simmer for 5 minutes. Remove from heat.

Add cheese and egg yolks and stir until blended. Beat egg whites with electric mixer until stiff. Stir ¼ of whites into vegetable mixture, stir and repeat three more times. Place hollowed-out peppers into an 8-inch baking pan and spoon filling evenly into each. Bake at 375°F for 35 minutes or golden brown and puffed.

"dibs on the extra egg yolk!" – tiamo

barks, giggles, grunts, growls and laughs

LASAGNA AL PESTO
Can be made one day in advance

1 lb. ricotta cheese
1½ c Parmesan cheese, grated
3 c shredded mozzarella cheese
½ c fresh parsley, minced
½ c green onions, minced
½ c pinon nuts
2-3 garlic cloves, minced
1 egg yolk
1½ tsp. fresh basil, minced
½ tsp. dried marjoram
salt to taste
freshly ground pepper to taste
¾ lb. lasagna noodles, cooked, rinsed in cold water and drained
pesto sauce (recipe on page 13)

Preheat oven to 350°F. Grease a shallow baking dish.

Combine all the ingredients except noodles, pesto sauce and 1 cup of mozzarella cheese. Blend well. Spread some of the filling over each lasagna noodle. Roll up jellyroll fashion. Stand vertically in the baking dish in a single layer.

Spoon pesto sauce over the top of each roll and sprinkle with the remaining 1 cup of mozzarella cheese.

Cover and bake for 30 to 40 minutes or until bubbly and heated through. Serve immediately.

"did someone say cheese?" - dolce

SHRIMP TACOS CON SMOKED CHIPOTLE PEPPERS
serve with beer and chips

2 tsp. chile powder
1 tsp. brown sugar
½ tsp. salt
½ tsp. ground cumin
¼ tsp. ground chile powder
1½ lbs. large uncooked shrimp, peeled and deveined
1 tsp. olive oil
2 tbsp. smoked chipotle peppers in adobo sauce, diced
8 white corn tortillas (6 inches)
2 c green cabbage, shredded
1 avocado, peeled and sliced
1 c jalapeno salsa – tends to be HOT
½ c cilantro, diced

Mix the first 5 ingredients in a large bowl. Add shrimp, stirring to coat the shrimp evenly.

Heat oil in a large nonstick skillet over medium-high heat. Add shrimp mixture to pan. Cook until shrimp turn slightly pink, about 3 minutes. DO NOT OVER COOK. Remove from heat.

Heat tortillas. Place two tortillas on a plate. Add four shrimp on each tortilla. Top with cabbage, avocado slices and 1-2 tbsp. salsa. Sprinkle top with cilantro.

Garnish with lime slices.

DRUNKEN CRANBERRY SAUCE
this will add a little kick to your holiday meal

1 – 10-oz. can crushed pineapple
12 oz. fresh cranberries
¾ c dark brown sugar
2 tbsp. fresh lemon juice
2 c water
6 oz. orange marmalade
¾ c Grand Marnier

Boil water, brown sugar and cranberries over high heat until cranberries pop, about 10 minutes. Pull off stovetop.

Add the rest of the ingredients and blend well. Refrigerate until cold (2 hours)
This stores for three weeks in the refrigerator.

Great on turkey sandwiches, pork chops and even toast.

"hmmm, i don't think i've had a cranberry before" - amore

POBLANO CHILES STUFFED WITH CRAB AND MANGO SALSA

1 c mango, peeled and chopped
1/3 c red bell pepper, chopped
2 tbsp. fresh cilantro, chopped
1 tbsp. white wine vinegar
3 tbsp. fresh Parmesan cheese, grated - divided
3 tbsp. fresh Romano cheese, grated – divided
1 tsp. dried oregano
1 tsp. Dijon mustard
¼ tsp. pepper
15 oz. fat-free ricotta cheese
1 – 14-oz. can artichoke hearts (packed in water), drained and chopped
8 oz. lump crabmeat
4 Poblano chiles, halved lengthwise and seeded
cilantro for garnish
lime slices for garnish

Combine first 4 ingredients in a small bowl. Stir well, cover and chill.

Preheat oven to 350°F. Combine 2 tbsp. Parmesan cheese, 2 tbsp. Romano cheese, oregano, mustard, pepper and ricotta cheese in a food processor. Blend until smooth. Spoon mixture in a bowl and stir in artichokes and crabmeat. Spoon mixture evenly in the chile halves and sprinkle with the remaining cheese. Place stuffed chiles on a baking sheet and bake for 30 minutes or until lightly browned.

Serve with mango salsa and garnish with cilantro and lime slices.

"i'll take some crab with that" - dolce

for the larger litter
when feeding the whole pack

When Tiamo was four weeks pregnant, we took her to the vet for an ultrasound. We were told she was going to have four puppies, but to our surprise, she had EIGHT! Here are some dishes for the larger crowd, for those meals when your dinner party grows, when the kids invite friends to stay over or when neighbors smell what's cooking.

chow time

POT ROAST

½ c all-purpose flour
1 tsp. salt
1 tsp. freshly ground pepper
4-6 lbs. beef chuck roast
2 tbsp. shortening
1 – 15-oz. jar horseradish (not processed)
12 small red potatoes, peeled and halved
8 medium carrots, peeled and chunked
8 onions, quartered
1 c water

Stir together flour, salt and pepper. Rub mixture on meat.

Melt shortening in large skillet. Place meat in skillet and brown over medium heat. Remove from heat and place roast in a prepared roasting pan, or a roasting bag.

Spread horseradish on top of roast. Add veggies and water. Cover tightly and bake in a preheated oven at 325°F for 4 hours.

"did we tell you we like carrots? raw or cooked, just push some over the edge of the cutting board to the floor – we'll do the rest. CRUNCH!" – the girls

BEEF STROGANOFF NEW MEXICO STYLE

3 onions, diced
4 garlic cloves, minced
2 tbsp. oil
1½ lbs. lean meat, cut into 1-inch cubes
½ c water
2 tsp. ground cumin
½ tsp. ground cinnamon
½ tsp. coriander
1 tsp. cayenne pepper
½ tsp. red pepper flakes
½ tsp. cardamom
1 – 28-oz. can chopped tomatoes

1½ c sour cream or plain yogurt

6 c cooked rice or noodles

Sauté onions and garlic in the oil. Add beef and simmer until brown. Add all other ingredients except the sour cream and rice. Cover tightly and simmer for 2 hours, stirring occasionally.

Stir some sauce into the sour cream, and then add sauce to the meat. Cook uncovered without boiling another 45 minutes.

Serve over rice.

"we loooove rice!" – tiamo, amore and dolce

ONE REASON WHY HE MARRIED ME PASTA

pasta always tastes better with a little butter and a whole lot of cheese!

1 c butter or olive oil
2 small onions, chopped
4 garlic cloves, chopped
8 oz. fresh mushrooms, sliced
1 c white wine
20 oz. angel-hair pasta
1 lb. cooked crispy bacon
grated Parmesan cheese to taste

Heat butter in small frying pan. Add onion and sauté until translucent. Add garlic and mushrooms and continue cooking until onion is slightly browned. Add wine and simmer, uncovered for 5 minutes.

Cook pasta according to package directions. Drain. Place pasta in serving dish and top with sauce. Sprinkle liberally with cheese and bacon and mix well.

Serve immediately.

"oh, please drop some bacon, oh, please drop some bacon!" — three wishful and hopeful girls

LEMON AND CREAM LINGUINE
is there anything better than pasta?

16 thin slices prosciutto, ham or bacon cut into strips
4 tbsp. butter
2 c chicken broth, low sodium
1 c heavy cream
½ c fresh lemon juice
8 tsp. lemon zest, finely grated
freshly ground pepper
1 c artichoke hearts (packed in water), chopped
1 lb. linguine
2 c Parmesan cheese

Sauté prosciutto in butter in a large sauté pan over medium heat. Add chicken broth and cook another minute.

Stir in cream, lemon juice and zest. Reduce heat to low and cook for 2-3 minutes. Season with pepper to taste. Remove from heat and cover to keep warm.

Prepare pasta according to package directions. Drain and transfer to the pan with the sauce. Stir over medium heat to incorporate into the sauce. Add the chopped artichokes and blend. Remove from the heat and stir in cheese. Transfer to a serving platter.

Garnish with lemon zest sprinkled over the top and serve with fresh, crusty farmer's bread.

WARNING: don't leave the cream carton on the counter. has been known to disappear.

CHILE CHEESE BAKE

2 – 4-oz. cans green chiles, diced
1 lb. Monterey Jack cheese, grated
1 lb. Cheddar cheese, grated
4 egg whites
4 egg yolks
½ c evaporated milk
1 tbsp. flour
½ tsp. salt
¼ tsp. pepper
3 tomatoes, thinly sliced
1 lb. cooked bacon

Preheat oven to 325°F. Butter a 9 inch x 13 inch glass baking dish. Combine green chiles and cheese in a large bowl. Place on the bottom of the baking dish.

Add flour and evaporated milk to the egg yolks. Set aside. Beat egg whites until stiff. Fold in egg whites to the flour mixture. Spread mixture over the cheese mixture in baking dish. Bake for 30 minutes.

Remove from oven and arrange the bacon and tomato slices on top of cheese mixture. Continue baking for another 30 minutes. Serve warm.

"ahhhh, cheeeeeese" - amore

the nose knows when something good is a'cookin'

SAUSAGE AND PEPPER CASSEROLE

serve along with some polenta, and dinner is served!

2 red bell peppers, thinly sliced
2 green bell peppers, thinly sliced
2 medium onions, thinly sliced
4-6 large garlic cloves, chopped
2 tsp. dried oregano
¼ tsp. dried crushed red pepper
2 tbsp. olive oil
2 lbs. hot Italian sausages

Preheat oven to 350°F. Combine first 5 ingredients in a 9 inch x 13 inch glass baking dish. Pour oil over ingredients and stir to coat. Season to taste with salt and pepper. Set aside.

Using tongs, brown sausages in a heavy nonstick skillet over high heat for about 6-7 minutes. Do not poke with a fork; you'll lose juices. Turn sausages often. Place on top of the pepper mixture.

Stirring occasionally, bake until sausages are cooked through and peppers and onions are tender, about 45 minutes.

Serve with hoagie rolls to make sandwiches.

"yum, yum, yum, sausages!" – the girls

precious!

chow for two

B.D. – Before dogs, my husband and I would enjoy intimate dinners for two. Candlelight combined with wine and grilled steaks with bleu cheese would be the weekend norm. These entrees are designed for small dinners or for two.

GRILLED FILET STEAKS WITH BLEU CHEESE
perfect for a special meal

2 – 2-inch thick filet steaks
4 oz. bleu cheese crumbles
4 oz. cream cheese
½ c green onions or green chile, chopped
4 slices bacon, thick cut
salt and pepper to taste

Cut a pocket in the side of each steak. Lightly season the steak with salt and pepper inside and outside. Set aside.

Mix the bleu cheese, cream cheese and green onion together. Spoon mixture into steak pocket (as full as possible). Wrap two bacon slices around the rim of the steak to cover the pocket, using toothpicks to secure the bacon ends.

Place on a prepared hot grill and cook to desired wellness.

Serve with a hearty red wine.

"damn husband! didn't leave any leftovers for us!" – the girls

VEAL SCALLOPS WITH DIJON MUSTARD SAUCE

6 veal scallops
1/3 c all-purpose flour
5 tbsp. butter

1 shallot, chopped
¼ c dry white wine
½ c whipping cream
2 tbsp. Dijon mustard

Flatten veal scallops to ¼-inch thickness. Lightly season flour with salt and pepper. Dredge veal in flour mixture. Melt 1 tbsp. butter in heavy skillet over medium heat. Add 2 veal scallops and cook until golden, approximately 2 minutes per side. Transfer to plate and keep warm. Repeat with remaining veal scallops using 1 tbsp. butter per batch.

Melt remaining 1 tbsp. butter in same skillet. Add shallot and sauté until softened. Add wine and bring to a boil. Scrape sides and any browned bits as you stir occasionally. Mix in cream. Bring to a boil, stirring constantly. Remove from heat and mix in mustard. You may season with salt and pepper to taste.

Pour sauce over veal and serve.

"where did that carton of cream go?" - tiamo

CRUNCHY PORK CHOPS

2 – 8-oz. boneless pork chops, trimmed of fat
1 large egg
½ tsp. Dijon mustard
¼ tsp. dried oregano
salt and pepper to taste
1 c fine dry breadcrumbs
1 tbsp. Parmesan, grated
cooking oil

Flatten pork chops until ½-inch thick. In a wide shallow bowl, combine the egg, mustard, oregano, and salt and pepper to taste. In another bowl, combine breadcrumbs and Parmesan.

Press each pork chop in the egg mixture, coating each side. Then dip each chop in the crumb mixture, covering the chop evenly. Set aside on a plate.

Add oil to a large skillet and place over medium heat. Place pork chops in skillet and cook, turning once, until deep golden brown about 7 minutes per side.

"meat with some crunch! our favorite!" – dolce and amore

GRILLED FLANK STEAK
Tougher cuts of meat can still be tender and taste delicious if cooked and cut properly

1/4 c olive oil
6 large garlic cloves, minced
1 tbsp. fresh rosemary, chopped
1 to 1½ lb. flank steak

Score the flank steak diagonally, on both sides, against the grain of the fiber with a sharp knife, making sure not to cut through the steak to the other side. Scoring the meat will help tenderize the cut and allows the meat to more easily absorb the marinade. Place in a large Ziploc plastic bag and set aside.

Whisk oil, garlic and rosemary together. Pour into the Ziploc bag and reseal. Place in the refrigerator overnight, occasionally turning the bag over to coat the other side.

Prepare grill at medium-high heat. Remove steak from marinade and sprinkle with salt and pepper. Grill steak until cooked to desired wellness, about 4 – 5 minutes per side for medium-rare. Transfer steak to platter and thinly slice on the diagonal across the grain.

"grrrr! mine! back off! don't even think about taking a bite!" - dolce

TILAPIA WITH MUSHROOMS

4 tsp. olive oil, divided
4 garlic cloves, finely minced
1 lb. button mushrooms, sliced
¼ c pitted green olives with juice, halved
2 c grape tomatoes, halved
1 tbsp. fresh thyme, chopped
1 tbsp. fresh basil, chopped
4 skinless tilapia filets
salt and pepper to taste

Heat 2 tsp. olive oil in large nonstick skillet over medium-high heat. Add garlic and mushrooms. Sauté for about 5 minutes. Stir and cook another 5 minutes. Add olives, tomatoes and herbs and cook another 2 minutes, until juice is evaporated. Remove from heat and place in a bowl. Cover to keep warm.

In same sauté pan, heat remaining olive oil over medium heat. Lightly season tilapia with salt and pepper. Place tilapia in sauté pan and cook for 3-4 minutes until nicely browned. Gently turn fish and cook another 3 minutes. Return vegetables and herbs to skillet to warm.

"we do fish" – tiamo, amore and dolce

grrrr! mine! back off!

PIZZA FOR TWO

GORGONZOLA AND TOMATO PIZZA

1 – 16-oz. package pizza dough
2 tbsp. olive oil
½ tsp. kosher salt
1 tbsp. cornmeal
¾ c shredded mozzarella cheese
½ c Gorgonzola cheese crumbles

2 beefsteak tomatoes, thinly sliced
2 tbsp. fresh basil, chopped
2 garlic cloves, minced
¼ tsp. salt
¼ tsp. crushed red pepper

Coat baking sheet with olive oil and sprinkle with salt and cornmeal. Place rolled-out pizza dough on baking sheet.

Sprinkle cheeses evenly over dough. Arrange tomato slices in a single layer over cheese. Combine basil and remaining ingredients in a bowl; sprinkle mixture over tomatoes. Bake in a preheated oven at 450°F for 12 minutes or until crust is golden brown.

SHRIMP SCAMPI PIZZA

1 – 16-oz. package pizza dough
3 tbsp. olive oil
3 tbsp. unsalted butter
4 cloves garlic, chopped

1 lb. medium-sized shrimp, peeled and
  deveined
¼ tsp. each salt and pepper
2 c shredded mozzarella cheese

Coat baking sheet with olive oil and sprinkle with salt and cornmeal. Place rolled-out pizza dough on baking sheet.

In a large skillet, heat butter and olive oil over medium-high heat. Add garlic and shrimp. Cook and stir about 2-3 minutes or until shrimp is just turning pink. Remove from the heat. Sprinkle with salt and pepper. Push shrimp to one side of the skillet.

Brush pizza crust with some of the butter-oil mixture from the shrimp pan. Arrange shrimp over crust evenly and sprinkle with mozzarella cheese. Bake at 425°F for 10 minutes or until top is lightly browned.

is there any for us?

momma knows best
good ol' comfort food

Everyone has that special comfort food that brings warm memories of mom. Sometimes, just the aroma of meatloaf will trigger those cozy feelings. Pasta, meatloaf and grilled cheese sandwiches are my comfort foods. Growing up, we were allowed to eat dinner in front of the TV on Sunday nights. Mom would make a big pot of spaghetti and we would slurp the noodles while watching the Wonderful World of Disney. To this day, pasta is my go-to food when I'm feeling blue.

momma time - tiamo and dolce

MEATLOAF AND LOAF

1 sourdough bread loaf (unsliced), hollowed out, saving the inside bread
1 – 3-oz. can mushrooms and liquids
1 egg, slightly beaten
½ c milk
1½ tsp. Worcestershire sauce
1 tsp. salt
1½ c soft breadcrumbs from sourdough bread loaf
2 tbsp. steak sauce
1½ lbs. lean ground beef
1 tsp. dry mustard
1 onion, diced
Tabasco sauce to taste

In large mixing bowl, combine liquids, egg, Worcestershire sauce, steak sauce, seasonings and breadcrumbs. Let stand for 5 minutes. Stir in beef, mushrooms, onions and Tabasco.

Fill the sourdough bread loaf with the meatloaf mixture.   Bake in a preheated oven at 350°F for 1 hour.

"what will it take to have some hamburger dropped over the edge of the counter?" – tiamo, amore, dolce

guarding the stash of goods!

FOUR CHEESE ZITI
i.e., fancy mac 'n' cheese

1 tbsp. butter, unsalted
½ c fresh breadcrumbs
1 lb. dry ziti pasta, prepared according to package directions
½ stick butter, unsalted
½ c Fontina cheese, diced
½ c Asiago cheese, diced
½ c mozzarella cheese, grated
½ c Parmesan cheese, grated
½ c heavy cream
¼ tsp. ground nutmeg
salt and pepper to taste

Toast the crumbs in 1 tbsp. butter until golden. Set aside.

Prepare the ziti according to the package directions. Drain. Stir in ½ stick butter until pasta is well coated.

Sprinkle the Fontina, Asiago and mozzarella cheeses over the top of the pasta. Cover and warm over low heat for 2-3 minutes, stirring vigorously to melt the cheeses. Stir in Parmesan cheese, cream, nutmeg, salt and pepper.

Arrange in a 9 inch x 13 inch casserole dish and bake at 350°F to heat through, about 20 minutes.

Sprinkle breadcrumbs over the top.

"cheese?" - tiamo

playtime with momma

FRIED ONION RINGS – NEW MEXICO STYLE

4 c vegetable oil
3 c all-purpose flour
2 tsp. cayenne pepper
2 tsp. red chile flakes
2 tsp. each salt and pepper
2 large onions, cut into thin rings

Preheat oven to 200°F. Heat oil to 350°F. Mix flour, cayenne, red chile, salt and pepper. Add a handful of onion rings and toss to coat. Remove excess flour from rings.

Add rings to oil and cook until golden brown, about 2-3 minutes. Transfer to paper towels to drain off extra oil. Keep warm in oven. Repeat with remaining rings and flour.

Let the husband clean up the oil splattered mess.

SPICY FRENCH FRIES

2 large potatoes, cut into thin strips
2 medium egg whites
¾ tsp. ground cumin
½ tsp. salt
½ tsp. chile powder
¼ tsp. freshly ground pepper

Preheat oven to 425°F. Spray a baking sheet with nonstick cooking spray. Combine all ingredients in a large bowl and toss to coat. Transfer to the baking sheet.

Bake the potatoes until just barely tender, about 15 minutes. Increase oven temperature to broil. Broil until crispy, about 10 minutes. Serve while still hot.

WARNING: Dogs love French fries!

playing in the snow – dolce and amore

JUST A GOOD OL' HASH CASSEROLE

2 tbsp. butter
5 mushrooms, chopped
2 shallots, chopped
1 celery stalk, chopped
½ large red bell pepper, chopped
2 medium potatoes, boiled, peeled and chopped
6 oz. cooked beef, diced in small pieces
¼ tsp. each salt and pepper
¼ c beef stock
2 tbsp. fresh parsley, chopped

Soak the potatoes in water for 30 minutes prior to mixing into the casserole.

Melt the butter in a skillet. Add the mushrooms, shallots, celery and bell pepper, stirring often until barely soft, about 5 minutes. Stir in the potatoes and meat. Season with salt and pepper and continue cooking until hash begins to sizzle, 3-4 minutes.

Pour in the beef broth. Cook over low heat for another 10 minutes, turning the hash over frequently. Cook, uncovered, until liquid evaporates and crust begins to form on bottom.

Sprinkle parsley on top when ready to serve.

"celery has some good crunch" - amore

SANTA FE RICE CASSEROLE

2 – 4-oz. cans green chile, diced
2 jalapeno, seeded and diced
3 c sour cream
3 c cooked rice
3 c Monterey Jack cheese, grated
2 c Cheddar cheese, grated
salt and pepper to taste
paprika

Mix chile and jalapeno with sour cream. Lightly season cooked rice with salt and pepper.

In a 2-quart casserole dish, layer the ingredients with rice, then sour cream mixture and Monterey Jack cheese. Repeat the layers, ending with rice on the top.

Bake at 350°F for 25 minutes. Cover the top with the Cheddar cheese and sprinkle with paprika. Bake another 5-10 minutes.

"drop the rice! now!" - tiamo

GRILLED CHEDDAR AND TOMATO SANDWICHES

the combination of cheddar and tomato is simply the best

8 bacon slices, thick cut + one extra slice to nibble on

8 sourdough bread slices, cut on the diagonal
2 c extra-sharp Cheddar cheese, grated
8 tomato slices, seeds removed
4 tbsp. mayonnaise

Cook bacon in heavy, large skillet over medium heat until brown and crispy. Transfer bacon to paper towels and drain excess grease.

Place 4 bread slices on a work surface and press ¼ cup grated cheese onto each slice. Top with 2 tomato slices on each bread slice. Sprinkle with pepper. Place 2 bacon slices atop each, breaking into pieces if necessary to fit. Press ¼ cup grated cheese over bacon on each. Top sandwiches with remaining bread slices. Spread ½ tbsp. mayonnaise on top of each top-tiered sandwich slice.

Heat a heavy skillet over medium heat. Add two sandwiches at a time, mayonnaise side down to the skillet. Cook sandwiches until bottom is golden brown – about 3 minutes. Spread ½ tbsp. of remaining mayonnaise on the top of each sandwich and flip over, mayonnaise side down. Cook until golden brown. Transfer sandwiches to work surface, cut in half and serve.

Other great grilled cheese combinations are: Cheddar and apple, Gouda and ham, Brie and ham, Fontina and roasted red pepper, and mozzarella and sausage.

WARNING: do not leave unattended; beware of four-legged sandwich thieves

amore

the dog pile
all the fun stuff!

As kids, we all played "dog pile". This section is for the miscellaneous fun stuff! There are butters, sauces, vinegars, jams, curds and some seriously addicting Spiced Pecans along with can't-just-have-one Peanut Butter Chocolate Balls. These recipes give that extra dash of spice at each dinner, bring just the right addition to the meal and add the special touches to the table.

wink, wink!

BUTTER UPS

LEMON DIJON BUTTER

½ c unsalted butter, softened
2 tsp. fresh lemon juice
2 tsp. parsley, minced
¼ tsp. salt
1/8 tsp. freshly ground pepper
2 tbsp. Dijon mustard

BASIL GARLIC BUTTER

½ c salted butter, softened
4 garlic cloves, minced and sautéed until golden
½ c fresh basil leaves, finely chopped
1 tsp. Dijon mustard
1 tsp. lemon peel, grated

FIERY PEPPER BUTTER

1/2 c unsalted butter, softened
1 – 7-oz. jar roasted bell peppers
1 tbsp. tomato paste
salt to taste

1½ tsp. brown sugar, firmly packed
¼ tsp. cayenne pepper
¼ tsp. hot pepper sauce

Combine ingredients for each butter. Cover and refrigerate before serving.
Makes about ½ cup for each butter. Let stand at room temperature before serving.
Great on sourdough bread, steaks and pasta.

WARNING: do not be surprised to find dog counter-surfing for butter. will break butter plate. will not care.

RASPBERRY RHUBARB JAM

6 c fresh unsweetened rhubarb, sliced
4 c brown sugar
3 c raspberry juice
2 c fresh raspberries
1 – 3-oz. pkg. raspberry-flavored gelatin

In a large kettle, combine the rhubarb, sugar and raspberry juice. Let stand for 15 minutes until the sugar is moistened. Bring to a boil for 10 minutes, uncovered, stirring frequently.

Add raspberries and return to a boil. Boil hard for 5-6 minutes or until it thickens, stirring frequently. Remove from heat and add the gelatin, stirring until dissolved.

Ladle mixture into half-pint containers, leaving some headspace on the top. Set stand at room temperature several hours until the jam has set.

Store in the refrigerator or freezer.

EASY-PEASY LEMON CURD

6 egg yolks, beaten
1 c sugar
½ c lemon juice, freshly squeezed

1 stick butter, cut in small pieces
2 tbsp. packed lemon zest

Whisk egg yolks, sugar and lemon juice together in a 4-cup measuring glass. Microwave at 70 percent power for 1 minute and then whisk the mixture. Microwave for another minute and whisk again. Microwave again for 2 minutes and whisk again. Continue to microwave mixture until it coats the back of a wooden spoon. Remove from microwave and stir in butter, one piece at a time. Add zest and stir well. Let cool.

Great on scones, biscuits, ice cream, shortbread cookies and as a filling for cakes or small tarts.

SAUCY SAUCES

HOLLANDAISE SAUCE

3 egg yolks
2 tbsp. fresh lemon juice
dash of salt
10 drops Tabasco sauce
½ c butter, melted
1 tsp. Dijon mustard

Combine the first 4 ingredients in a blender. Blend until smooth. Add butter a little at a time and then add mustard. Blend thoroughly. Serve immediately.

SAUTERNE ARTICHOKE DIPPING SAUCE

1 c sauterne
3 tbsp. onion, minced
2 c mayonnaise
3 tbsp. parsley, chopped
3 tbsp. fresh lemon juice
1 egg, beaten

Mix all together and heat slowly. Use to dip artichoke leaves.

CRÈME DIJON SAUCE

1/3 c Dijon mustard
2 eggs, beaten
1 c whipping cream

1 tbsp. vinegar
¼ tsp. tarragon

In a small saucepan, combine all ingredients, stirring until smooth. Cook over low heat, stirring constantly until mixture begins to thicken.

Great over pork chops, chicken and vegetables.

COCKTAIL SAUCE

¾ c chile sauce
3 tbsp. fresh lemon juice
3 tbsp. prepared horseradish
2 tsp. Worcestershire sauce
½ tsp. onion flakes
dash of Tabasco sauce, to taste

Mix well. Add salt to taste and chill.

"forget the sauce, we just want the shrimp!" – the girls

BAR-B-QUE SAUCE

1 – 8-oz. can tomato paste
½ c A-1 steak sauce
½ c oil
1/3 c brown sugar, firmly packed
2 tbsp. vinegar

Mix well and chill.

CREAMY HORSERADISH SAUCE

1 tbsp. butter
1 tbsp. shallot, minced
2 tsp. garlic, minced
1 c dry white wine
1 tsp. lemon juice

1 c sour cream
½ c prepared horseradish
1 tbsp. green onion, minced
1 tbsp. fresh thyme, minced

Melt butter and add shallots and garlic. Sauté until soft, add wine and simmer until reduced to 2 tbsp. Remove from heat and cool. Whisk remaining ingredients into shallot mixture. Cover and refrigerate.

"we'll take steak with that!" – tiamo, amore and dolce

CRANBERRY VINEGAR

1 – 12 oz. bag fresh cranberries
3 c white vinegar
1 – 750 ml bottle champagne (3½ c)
additional fresh cranberries

In a large stainless-steel saucepan, combine the cranberries, vinegar and champagne. Bring to a boil and reduce the heat. Simmer uncovered for 3 to 5 minutes. Remove from heat and cool completely. Cover tightly with plastic wrap and a tight-fitting lid and let stand in a cool, dark place for two weeks.

Strain the vinegar and champagne mixture and discard the cranberries. Transfer to a decorative bottle. At this point, you may add some additional cranberries to each bottle. Store up to six months. Use in your favorite salad dressing recipes.

ROSEMARY WINE VINEGAR

1 c fresh rosemary sprigs, tightly packed
4 tiny hot peppers, such as cayenne or jalapeno
6 c white wine vinegar
additional fresh rosemary sprigs

Rinse the rosemary sprigs and pat dry. In a large stainless-steel saucepan, combine the rosemary sprigs, hot peppers and vinegar. Crush the rosemary lightly with the back of a spoon. Bring almost to a boil and remove from the heat, cooling completely. Pour mixture into a 2-quart jar and cover tightly with plastic wrap and then a tight-fitting lid. Let stand in a cool, dark place for two weeks.

Strain the vinegar, discarding the rosemary and peppers. Transfer mixture to decorative bottles, adding a sprig of fresh rosemary to each bottle.

"Vinegar! Uck!" – the girls

full of "@#$(%" and vinegar!

ADDICTION

SPICED PECANS

1 lb. pecan halves
1 egg white
1 tbsp. amaretto
1 c dark brown sugar
1 tsp. salt
1 tsp. cinnamon

Preheat oven to 300°F. Beat egg white with amaretto until you barely have soft peaks. Add sugar, salt and cinnamon. Mix in pecans and stir until pecans are completely coated. Place on a well-greased baking sheet. Bake for 40 minutes, stirring every 10 minutes. Cool completely and store in the freezer.

PEANUT BUTTER CHOCOLATE BALLS

½ c unsalted butter
2 c cornflakes cereal
2 c creamy peanut butter (do not use old-fashioned or freshly ground)
2 c powdered sugar
1 tbsp. Kahlua
1 c brown sugar
15 oz. semisweet chocolate, chopped

Line baking sheet with foil. Melt butter in heavy saucepan over low heat. Combine cornflakes, peanut butter, powdered sugar and brown sugar in a bowl. Mix in butter and Kahlua. Moisten hands and roll 1 tablespoon of mixture into a ball. Place on prepared baking sheet. Repeat with remaining mixture and chill overnight.

Melt chocolate in a double boiler over low heat, stirring occasionally. Remove from heat. Using a fork, dip peanut butter balls one at a time into chocolate and transfer to a foil-lined cookie sheet. Refrigerate until chocolate is firm.

WARNING: seriously addicting - keep away from husbands and dogs

also addicting: cute puppies

eat veggies last
they don't need as much room

Most vegetable dishes are what they call "side dishes" I say, push them to the side (and over the edge) so there is plenty of room for the good stuff. As a caterer, I found veggies were usually what would be left on the plate. It became a challenge to create a vegetable dish so appealing and delicious that the most die-hard vegetable haters would eat their veggies. It can be a challenge to get adults to eat their greens, let alone a child, but it's not a problem for Tiamo, Amore and Dolce. The trick is not to let your husband see you feeding the dogs at the dinner table.

dolce

ROASTED ASPARAGUS

1 lb. fresh asparagus
1 red bell pepper
3-4 garlic cloves, minced
sea salt and pepper
olive oil

Prep the asparagus by snapping off the ends at the breaking point. Slice the red bell pepper into narrow strips approximately 3-4 inches in length. Combine the asparagus, pepper strips and garlic and coat with olive oil. Place in the bottom part of a broiler pan. Sprinkle sea salt and pepper on asparagus to taste.

Turn the broiler on to high. Broil the asparagus until just starting to brown. You may stir the asparagus while broiling to even the cooking.

Best with thin stalks.

"we eat the leftover stalks; they're a bit chewy, but still good" – tiamo, amore and dolce

GRILLED CORN ON THE COB WITH JALAPENO BUTTER

8 ears of corn
½ c butter, room temperature
1/3 c fresh chives, finely chopped
2 jalapeno peppers, finely chopped with seeds
1 tsp. grated lime peel
½ sea salt
¼ tsp. paprika
Tabasco sauce to taste
pinch of cayenne pepper to taste

Mix the butter, chives, peppers, lime peel, salt, paprika, Tabasco and cayenne pepper together in a bowl. Set aside.

Peel back the corn husks (leaving husks attached) and remove the silk from the corn. Fold husks back into place to cover the corn. Soak in water to moisten the husks.

Prepare the grill. Once hot, place corn on grill to cook, turning often. Grill until husks are slightly charred and corn is tender. About 10-15 minutes.

Serve with jalapeno butter.

"butter! good!" - dolce

BRUSSELS SPROUTS WITH PINE NUTS

1½ lbs. Brussels Sprouts
2 tbsp. pine nuts
2 tbsp. butter
¼ c shallots, chopped
2 tbsp. currants, golden works well
½ tsp. fresh thyme, chopped
1 tsp. sea salt
¼ tsp. freshly ground black pepper
½ c chicken broth

Cut off the bottom stems of the sprouts and discard.

Heat a large nonstick skillet over medium-high heat. Add nuts to pan and cook about two minutes. Set aside the nuts. Melt butter in pan; add shallots, and sauté for 1 minute. Stir in Brussels Sprouts, currants, thyme, salt and pepper. Toss to combine. Add broth. Cover and reduce heat, cooking for another 7 minutes.

Increase heat to medium-high, uncover and cook another 5 minutes or until liquid evaporates and sprouts are tender.

Remove from heat and sprinkle with pine nuts.

"we really don't care for these; give 'em to someone else" – the girls

dolce

GREEN BEANS WITH BACON

the girls love the crunch of the green bean tips if they happen to drop to the floor!

½ lb. green beans, trimmed and cut into 2-inch lengths
3 bacon slices
1 tbsp. shallot, chopped
2 tsp. white wine vinegar

Cook green beans in large pot of boiling salted water until tender, about 8-10 minutes. Drain and transfer to a shallow serving bowl.

Cook bacon in medium skillet until crispy. Drain on paper towels to absorb excess grease.

Add shallot to skillet and sauté 30 seconds. Remove from heat and cool slightly. Stir vinegar into shallot mixture in skillet. Season warm dressing with salt and pepper.

Pour dressing over green beans and toss to coat. Crumble bacon on top and serve warm.

"bacon! i'm in heaven!" - amore

happy amore

GARDENER'S CASSEROLE
a veggie lover's nirvana

4 small zucchini, sliced crosswise ¼-inch thick
2 tomatoes, diced
1 carrot, sliced crosswise very thin
1 celery stalk, sliced diagonally ¼-inch thick
1 red bell pepper, chopped
1 banana pepper, finely chopped (optional)
½ onion, coarsely chopped
½ c chicken broth
4 bacon slices
3 c sharp Cheddar cheese, grated

salt and pepper to taste

Preheat the oven to 350°F. Combine the vegetables, chicken broth and half of the cheese in a mixing bowl. Season with salt and pepper to taste. Place in a greased casserole dish.

Cover and bake for 1 hour. Check the carrots for tenderness, using a fork. Top with the bacon slices and sprinkle the remaining cheese over the bacon. Return to the oven to cook another 30 to 45 minutes.

"we'll take the zucchini, tomatoes, carrots, and celery. you may keep the peppers and onions" - amore and dolce

hell bent for leather

ZUCCHINI HASH BROWNS
a breakfast delight!

4 c zucchini, grated
½ tsp. salt
2 eggs, beaten
6 tbsp. Parmesan cheese, grated
2 garlic cloves, finely minced
salt and pepper to taste
4 tbsp. butter, divided

Mix grated zucchini with salt. Let stand 15 minutes. Squeeze with hands to press out excess moisture. Stir beaten eggs into zucchini. Add cheese, garlic, salt and pepper. Combine well.

Melt half of the butter in a skillet over medium heat. When butter is hot, spoon zucchini mixture into skillet in 2-tbsp.-sized mounds. Flatten with the back of a wooden spoon. Sauté uncovered until golden brown, turning once, about 4 minutes per side.

Transfer patties to a warm platter and repeat with the remaining zucchini mixture. Add remaining butter as needed.

Serve immediately while still hot.

"drop a little egg this way" – tiamo

dolce – basking in the sun

TOMATO POTS

4 medium tomatoes, halved
¼ tsp. salt
¼ tsp. pepper
1 garlic clove, minced
1 medium onion, minced
3 tbsp. breadcrumbs
4 oz. bleu cheese, crumbled

Cut tomatoes in half crosswise. Gently press out juice and seeds. Sprinkle with salt and pepper. Place tomatoes in a muffin tin. Combine garlic and onions. Divide evenly over tomatoes. Combine breadcrumbs and cheese. Sprinkle over tomatoes. Bake tomatoes at 350°F for 20-25 minutes or until tomatoes are just turning tender. May also broil 5 minutes until cheese is light brown and tomatoes are heated through. Carefully remove from muffin tin and place on serving platter.

GREEN BEAN BUNDLES

2 lbs. green beans, trimmed
1 red bell pepper, cut in ¼-inch-thick strips
1 yellow bell pepper, cut into ¼-inch strips
8 green onions

1/3 c butter
2 garlic cloves, minced
½ tsp. thyme
¼ tsp. white pepper

Boil the green onions whole until just barely tender. Remove from the hot water and set aside. Add the beans to the hot water and boil until tender, about 15 minutes. Drain and let cool slightly. Divide green beans into 8 bundles. Wrap a green onion stem around each bundle and tie in a knot, holding the beans together. Insert 3 to 4 strips of bell pepper in the bundle. Place in a casserole dish. Melt butter, garlic, thyme and pepper together and drizzle over green bean bundles. Bake for 10 minutes at 350°F.

"I love green beans!"

the daily dog things we dooo!

is it morning yet? jump on mom to wake her up, go out to the pen to see if anything happened overnight, eat, get newspaper, wag tail, take a nap, chew up a book, sigh, check to see if there is anything new in the dog bowl, rats! take a nap, roll over and stretch, emit a dog fart, sigh, head bump malcolm for a quick rub on the ears, wag tail, take another nap, wake up barking at a noise, sigh, counter-surf for crumbs - rats! nothing - sigh, bug malcolm, bark some more, eat, check out the kitchen floor — something new might have fallen from the counter, rats! nothing - sigh, tear through the house to the outdoor pen, track dirt back in the house, beg for a doggie treat, wag tail, sigh, bark some more, plop down and sigh, when is megs coming home from work, sigh, fart, bark at a car driving by, do another drive-by in the kitchen - rats! nothing - go for a walk with malcolm - yippee! - get home and take another nap, wag tail, eat, burp, fart, run through the house and slide on the rug - yippee! - megs is home - yippee! — wag tail a lot, let's go give her a welcome attack, bark, bark, bark, bark, beg for another dog snack, take a nap, follow megs and malcolm around the house from room to room, wag tail, is it bedtime yet? put head back down, now it's time, jump on bed and curl up to megs, cuddle, get scratched, roll over for a belly rub, get scratched, cuddle, nudge amore over so dolce can get closer, get dog hair all over the expensive down pillows, stretch, one last cuddle, ohhh siiiiggghh —

good night y'all!

heading home

Bernese Mountain Dogs

The Bernese Mountain Dog is one of four varieties of the Swiss Mountain Dog. Bernese Mountain Dogs originated in Switzerland and are named for the Canton of Bern. Their deep-barreled chest is perfect for drafting. They were used as working farm dogs, bred to pull carts loaded with heavy milk cans to the dairy, watch and drive cow herds to and from their pastures and be the Farmer's companion. Bernese Mountain Dogs are hardy and thrive in cold weather. Their intelligence, strength and agility were ideal for general farm work. They make great watch dogs but are not necessary guard dogs.

Not long ago, the Bernese Mountain Dogs were a relatively rare breed. They were rescued from near extinction by Professor Albert Heim in the early 1900's and have slowly developed since then. Berners are known to have arrived in America around 1926 but were not recognized by the AKC until 1937. Since then the breed's popularity has been on the rise.

Bernese Mountain Dogs are strikingly beautiful dogs. With their tri-colored coat and their gentle and pleasant disposition, they make an ideal companion dog. The breed has a large sturdy frame and is usually calm, and self-confident. They are good-natured and never sharp or shy but may remain placid or aloof to the attentions of strangers. They are a great fit for families.

Berners needs lots of human companionship and should be considered a full member of the family. They are very good with other animals and children. Berners have long, shining coats that can be straight or slightly wavy. They require regular grooming as they trend to shed due to their double-coat. Berners need moderate activity such as daily walks. Plan on enjoying your Berner ALL the time, as they are not a breed to be ignored or left alone for long periods of time.

dolce

Special Tail Wags

To me, all the slicing, dicing, mixing, fixing, baking, making, roasting, toasting, blending, rending, frying, trying, chopping and dropping is in preparation of gathering my favorite people together around the dinner table to share in our bounty and our lives.

Cooking is about true friends who are happy to share in the simplest of meals and never mind the dogs underfoot and under the table. It's about the special camaraderie between sisters and sister-like-friends when "doing the dishes" after supper. It's about leftovers and swapping recipes and planning the next get-together.

Special tail wags go out to Alex and Celia Marshall, Jim and Darlene Garton, Walter Cooper and Doug Bland, Dick and Terri Johnson, and Jonnalyn Grover and John Johnson. A little wine, a big dinner, a lot of laughs, a lot of reminiscing, I thank you for your gift of friendship.

Special tail wags to Ms. Tara Garton. Dog washer extraordinaire, superb puppy sitter and dog watcher, you tended and cared for our girls as if they were you own. You, my beautiful dear, are very, very special!

Special tail wags to Dr. Sue McKelvey and Dr. Bob Gruda. The best vets ever! You rock!

To our neighbors and neighborhood, you've put up with those "crazy" dog people all these years – thank you for your forbearance.

And to my dear husband, Malcolm…

When Malcolm and I were first married, we lived in a tiny little house with a tinier little kitchen. We bumped elbows on more than one occasion while working in the kitchen together. We shared counter space along with kitchen duty, sampled and savored each other's skills in the scullery, and tossed a coin to see who would do that night's dinner dishes. While instructing my husband on how to correctly chop the parsley or how to roast a pork loin, he in turn, taught me how to open my heart to all his love. For every time I showed him how to properly slice an onion or how to sharpen a knife, Malcolm has shown me his forever loving support and his continuing encouragement. If I coached him in prepping veggies, Malcolm tutored me to take risks, always there by my side, always there to steady me if I stumbled. I might have exposed Malc to new recipes and interesting dishes – Malcolm uncovered a whole new world of experiences for me to cherish and hold dear. Over dinner and dishes, Malcolm has given me unconditional love and unwavering support. There aren't enough tail wags to express my love for you.

Tiamo
November 2005 – May 2012

you will always be our "girl"

Index

21885553R00098

Made in the USA
Charleston, SC
06 September 2013